Octavio Paz

Titles in the series Critical Lives present the work of leading cultural figures of the modern period. Each book explores the life of the artist, writer, philosopher or architect in question and relates it to their major works.

In the same series

Michel Foucault
David Macey

James Joyce
Andrew Gibson

Jean Genet
Stephen Barber

Noam Chomsky
Wolfgang B. Sperlich

Pablo Picasso
Mary Ann Caws

Jorge Luis Borges
Jason Wilson

Franz Kafka
Sander L. Gilman

Erik Satie
Mary E. Davis

Guy Debord
Andy Merrifield

Georges Bataille
Stuart Kendall

Frank Lloyd Wright
Robert McCarter

Ludwig Wittgenstein
Edward Kanterian

Octavio Paz

Nick Caistor

REAKTION BOOKS

Published by Reaktion Books Ltd
33 Great Sutton Street
London EC1V ODX, UK

 www.reaktionbooks.co.uk

First published 2007

Printed and bound in Slovenia
by MKT PRINT d.d.

British Library Cataloguing in Publication Data
Caistor, Nick
    Octavio Paz. – (Critical lives)
    1. Paz, Octavio, 1914–98   2. Poets, Mexican – 20th century –
    Biography
    I. Title
    861.6'2

ISBN-13: 978 1 86189 303 1
ISBN-10: 1 86189 303 5

Contents

Introduction   7

1 Finding a Voice, 1914–37   12

2 Taking a Stand, 1937–43   33

3 New Departures, 1943–53   54

4 Reaching Out, 1953–69   77

5 Bringing it all Back Home, 1969–90   100

6 Consuming Fires, 1990–98   118

References   127

Select Bibliography   136

Acknowledgements   143

Photo Acknowledgements   144

Octavio Paz in his early seventies, in England.

Introduction

The poet and essayist Octavio Paz was born in 1914, under what he once called 'the twin black star' of the First World War and the continuing violence of the Mexican Revolution. In all his work he sought to define his own identity in response to the destruction and terror of twentieth-century history, while at the same time exploring his own biographical journey in the search for poetic expression. Whereas his near-contemporary, the Argentine writer Jorge Luis Borges, saw Latin America's distance from Europe and its traditions as giving him the freedom to play with those traditions without being bound to any one specific national representation of them, Paz was more deeply affected by the separation of Mexico from Europe. Mexicans spoke the language of Spain, and inherited its literature and thought, but they did so in a totally different context. They also had to contend with and respond to a very different historical process. Much of Paz's work is an attempt to define that divided Mexican identity, in prose works such as the 1950 *El laberinto de la soledad* and *Sor Juana Inés de la Cruz o las trampas de la fe* from the 1980s, as well as in many of his most eloquent poems. Other poems are a search for his place within the complex tradition he had inherited and, increasingly, as he grew older, an attempt to free the words he uses from their accepted, everyday meanings in order to create something new.

This striving for novelty was no narcissistic exercise. Paz was always convinced of the high seriousness of poetic endeavour, sharing Shelley's view that poets are 'the unacknowledged legislators of mankind'; he even told the Mexican president as much during his last public appearance at the opening of the Octavio Paz Foundation in Mexico City in 1997. In spirit he was most closely linked to the French Surrealist leader André Breton. Both men were convinced that literature was a moral adventure made even more important by the horrors of history, an adventure in which authenticity of behaviour and expression was the key to a reaffirmation of human freedom.

Paz's search for definitions of individual and national identity was also very different from that of Borges. Unlike the Argentine writer, who saw identity as constantly shifting and bordering on the indefinable, for Paz it implied a series of masks that needed to be stripped away to reveal the truth underneath. In his own life Paz had to contend with a double inheritance. On the one side were the powerful figures of his grandfather and father: the mixed, Mexican side of his identity, with all its complications. Europe was the maternal, female side: both his mother and his first wife, Elena Garro, were first-generation Mexicans of Spanish parents, while his second wife, Marie-José, was French. In a reversal of the historic 'rape' of Mexico by the Spaniards that he describes so powerfully in *El laberinto de la soledad*, in his own family it is the violent Mexican male who is linked to the submissive, all-suffering Spanish female.

Beyond his own family identity, Paz also constantly defined and redefined what he thought of Mexico and its place in the world. In his youth, the outcome of the revolution was still uncertain: he and many others thought it could be taken a step further, and become a new 'socialist' society that in some ways mirrored the model of the Soviet Union. But as the 1930s unfolded it became plain that Mexico was following a very different path. The creation and consolidation of the Partido Revolucionario Institucional (Institutional Revolutionary Party) produced something unique and ambiguous. Although he served his country for almost a quarter of a century in its foreign service, Paz constantly questioned the kind of regime it represented. Even when in his later years he became the grand old man of Mexican literature – in particular after becoming the only Mexican as yet to win the Nobel Prize for Literature – he continued to urge the PRI to push ahead with reforms that would make Mexico a more modern representative democracy.

These views, expressed in trenchant prose and in many public appearances, led to a running battle with the left-wing orthodoxies that Paz saw as dominating Mexican academic and intellectual life. He came to reject revolution as any kind of answer to the deep-seated problems not only of his own country, but of the rest of Latin America and the developing world. He did not see the inequalities of these societies as needing a violent overthrow: he wanted them to follow the path of democratic reform based on lucid criticism. He did not see himself as a conservative, but rather as someone who thought revolution came through the truth of poetry and individual revolt, although he was not confident that this could be anything more than a momentary glimpse of human brotherhood.

The arguments he constantly faced with the Mexican intelligentsia were part of a more general unease with his own country. He was one of the last 'men of letters', a writer who had not specialized in anything but his own poetry, and yet was convinced that the effort to make poetry also created the moral obligation to speak his mind on everything going on around him. He was a true amateur who insisted that nothing was beyond the scope of passionate enquiry. In interview, he always displayed a youthful enthusiasm for whatever topic was under discussion, bringing his own broad knowledge to bear and launching off into interrogations that came to his mind as he spoke, as though he were constantly approaching the matter for the first time. At the end of an interview, he would say: 'I hope this hasn't all been rather too superficial, has it?' The fluidity of inspiration also shone though in his essays and his poems: rarely has there been a more vivid and supple intelligence informing both genres.

At his death in 1998 Paz was lauded both inside Mexico and beyond as one of its greatest twentieth-century poets, as well as one of its most influential prose writers. Since then in his own country there has been a certain eclipse of his reputation. The 'academy' has moved on, and tried to forget him. The Octavio Paz Foundation, containing an invaluable collection of his papers, manuscripts, photographs and other material, had to close down when his widow Marie-José Tramini became concerned at the use being made of it by some Mexican academics. After more than seventy years, the PRI has been voted out of power in Mexico. The new Partido de Acción Nacional (National Action Party) has shown little taste for the kind of 'patrimonial' patronage that the old regime used to offer. It has preferred to leave Mexicans to the kind of 'facile hedonism' of which Paz was so critical, and has largely abandoned attempts to define a national character in favour of letting individuals seek their own identity as they see fit.

Octavio Paz once referred in interview to the story of Alexander the Great being asked which he would prefer to be: Achilles or Homer. Naturally enough, Alexander chose the Greek hero over what he called the mere 'trumpeter' of the other man's deeds. Paz dismissed this as absurd – for him as a poet and as a man who devoted his life to writing, it was far more important to bear witness to the events of history. And poetry itself was a presence, he felt, which in however small a way became a part of history itself. This was not a claim he made easily, however. In his book *La otra voz* ('The Other Voice') about the importance of the poetic voice, he poses the question that has disturbed the sleep of almost all twentieth century poets: 'Any reflection about poetry should begin, or end, with this question: who and how many read poetry books?'

Paz himself is one of only a handful of Latin American poets, alongside Pablo Neruda, César Vallejo and Nicolás Guillén, whose work is still present for the generation born at the end of a century that challenged the capacity of literature to have its own voice heard and not drowned out entirely by the destructive roar of history. Although deeply rooted in the complexities of Mexico and its identity, Paz's insistence that the pursuit of poetry represents an essential human value gives his work a resonance that crosses all borders.

1

Finding a Voice, 1914–37

Octavio Paz was born in Mexico City on 31 March 1914. In Europe this was the last spring of what many saw as a golden age brought to a tragic end when the First World War began later that year. In Mexico the revolutionary violence that had broken out in 1910 and swept away the long-standing dictator Porfirio Díaz in 1911 still engulfed the country, as different factions fought for power. A month after Octavio Paz Solórzano's birth American troops bombarded and then occupied the port of Veracruz, taking advantage of the continuing turmoil. A year earlier the centre of Mexico City had been engulfed in the fighting known as the 'ten tragic days' when rival groups lobbed shells and exchanged gunfire between the presidential palace and the nearby Ciudadela fortress. As many as five hundred civilians died, and President Francisco Madero was first arrested and then murdered. In the struggle for power that followed in 1914 the printer's shop in the heart of the old city that was owned and run by young Octavio's grandfather Ireneo Paz (1835–1924) was ransacked. Already in his eighties, the old man decided to move the family out of the city centre to more peaceful surroundings in Mixcoac, a small, pre-Columbian town then completely separate from the metropolis.

This grandfather on his father's side was a hugely powerful influence on the young Paz. He was the growing boy's direct link to the struggles for Mexican independence in the nineteenth century, in which he had personally played a significant role, and to Mexican history in general. Ireneo Paz was a lawyer and journalist who had supported the liberal revolution in the 1850s led by Benito Juárez, the 'Zapotec Indian from Oaxaca', who brought in Mexico's first Republican Constitution. He also fought in the army trying to prevent the French from installing Austrian Archduke Maximilian as emperor of Mexico in the 1860s, rising to the rank of colonel. But, despite his convinced nationalism, by the 1880s Ireneo supported the efforts of President Porfirio Díaz to modernize Mexico and open it to the world. He became a member of the Federal Congress, and was a prolific writer of historical novels, plays and a biography of Porfirio Díaz, as well as his own memoirs. As a novelist, he was one of the precursors of the 'indigenista' movement, which sought to make the indigenous inhabitants of Mexico protagonists of the national narrative for the first time. The awareness of the presence of the 'other', the silenced, marginalized voice of the country's first inhabitants, fascinated Octavio from an early age.

At the same time, the Paz household was open to outside influences. Despite his opposition to the French invasion, by the 1880s Ireneo Paz saw France as the emblem of modernity. In 1889 he even travelled to Paris as an exhibitor at the Exposition Universelle (of which the newly completed Eiffel Tower was the main attraction), where he displayed examples of his printing and binding.[1] Paz's grandfather brought back all the latest French literature to add to the classics in his vast library, and many years later he was to teach his young grandson to admire and respect French thought and literature. This francophilia was seconded by 'la tía Amalia', an eccentric maiden aunt who lived with the family and apparently encouraged the young boy to read Rousseau, Victor Hugo and Michelet as well as French children's authors. Octavio never forgot these lessons: as an adult, he lived in Paris for two very fruitful periods, and the childhood habit of reading in French continued throughout his life. To Paz, France was in many senses his intellectual home. When in 1989 he received the Alexis de

Tocqueville Prize personally from President François Mitterrand, he thanked him by saying 'French literature has always been my second spiritual home'.[2]

Critics have traced back Octavio Paz's combination of deeply felt nationalism with an unusual openness to other traditions and experiences to his grandfather's example. Whatever its origins, this attitude often brought the adult Octavio into conflict with left-wing Mexican intellectuals (from the 1930s to the 1990s) who thought that to be 'truly' Mexican meant to reject all foreign influences, and that they had to devote all their energies to creating a specifically 'Mexican' literature and art. Paz always refused to accept any narrow definitions of this kind. From his own family experience he was aware that to be Mexican involved a complicated inheritance, whilst his travels in the United States, Europe and the Far East led him to seek define his own culture in contrast to others, rather than to look for a 'telluric' authenticity (as 1930s nationalist literary groups in Mexico called it).

Whereas the young boy's grandfather seems to have been a benign if austere figure, his father, Octavio Paz Solórzano, Ireneo's youngest son, was a far more troubling influence. He too was a lawyer, but soon after the outbreak of the revolution in 1910 threw in his lot with Emiliano Zapata, the tempestuous leader of the revolutionary forces from the south of the country. Zapata was the revolutionary leader most committed to land reform, using force to expropriate many of the huge haciendas or ranches often owned by absentee landlords. In 1914 his troops occupied the capital (Zapata is said to have stayed only one night, complaining that the city was – even then – 'unfit for human habitation'). It was around this time that Paz's father joined up with him, working as a lawyer on land reform issues, and as Zapata's personal secretary. After the end of the revolutionary period in 1920, Octavio Paz senior continued to press for agrarian reform, and was a national deputy for the Partido Nacional Agrarista (National Agrarian Party). Partly because of this work he was absent from the family house for long

Zapatistas taking coffee at Sanborn's in Mexico City, 1915.

periods, and when he did return appears to have been a violent, disruptive presence.

Octavio Paz looked back on his childhood in poetry written some sixty years later. In a long poem first called 'Tiempo Adentro' ('Time Inside') and then 'Pasado en claro' (a typically multi-layered title, containing ideas of 'a fair copy of the past', and 'setting things straight'), Paz examines these early years and the ways in which he feels they created the writer in him. The epigraph from William Wordsworth's *The Prelude* makes this clear: 'Fair seed-time had my soul, and I grew up / Foster'd alike by beauty and by fear . . .'. His description of his father in this 1974 poem underlines the fearful aspect he brought to the youngster's early years:

> *Del vómito a la sed*
> *Atado al potro del alcohol,*
> *Mi padre iba y venía entre las llamas.*

From vomit to thirst
Stretched on the rack of alcohol
My father came and went amid flames.[3]

Another poem, this time from the 1960s, intercalated among the
thoughts and sensations that arose from living for several years in
India ('Ladera este' or 'Eastern Slope') discusses the influence of
both these male presences on his boyhood. Subtitled 'A Mexican
Song', possibly for the way it keeps coming back into his mind like
a refrain, the poem conjures up their voices and links the two older
men to action, danger, and the decisive moments of Mexican history:
the French invasion in the 1860s, the long and increasingly abusive
rule of Porfirio Díaz and the twentieth-century revolutionary leaders.
In contrast to their violent, adventurous lives, 'reeking of gunpowder',
Paz recalls his own uncertainties:

Mi abuelo al tomar el café
Me hablaba de Juárez y de Porfirio
Los zuavos y los plateados
Y el mantel olía a pólvora.
Mi padre, al tomar la copa
Me hablaba de Zapata y de Villa
Soto y Gama y los Flores Magón.
Y el mantel olía a pólvora.

Yo me quedo callado:
De quién podría hablar?

Over coffee, my grandfather
told me about Juárez and Porfirio
the zouaves and the Silver Band.
The tablecloth reeked of gunpowder.
Lifting his glass, my father

told me about Zapata and Villa
Soto y Gama and the Flores Magons.
The tablecloth reeked of gunpowder.

I had nothing to say:
Who did I have to talk about?[4]

Fifty years after living through scenes like these, this little poem
gives not only a strong sense of the young boy's loneliness and
isolation (accentuated by the fact of being an only child) but the
circumstances that may have given rise to his poetic voice. The
elder males in the family are the ones who have lived through the
turbulent years of recent Mexican history: but what experience
does the poet have to call on to make his own voice heard? Perhaps
this is the genesis of that 'other voice' of poetry on which the adult
Paz insisted so often: 'Poetry is the other voice. Not the voice of
history or of anti-history, but the voice which, in history, is always
saying something different.'[5]

Against these violent, energetic male presences stands Paz's
mother, Josefina Lozano. It was from her that Octavio inherited his
startling blue eyes. These early on earned him the nickname of the
'Visigoth', and also contributed to the young boy's feeling apart
from the dark-haired, dark-eyed, 'typical' Mexican. Born near Cádiz
in the south of Spain, Josefina appears to have been the rock for
the young boy's affections. The manner in which the adult Paz
describes her in *Pasado en claro* could not be more different from
the depiction of his father:

Mi madre, niña de mil años
Madre del mundo, huérfana de mí,
Abnegada, feroz, obtusa, providente,
Jilguera, perra, hormiga, jabalina,
Carta de amor con faltas de lenguaje,

Mi madre: pan que yo cortaba
Con su propio cuchillo cada día.

My mother, girl of a thousand years
Mother of the world, orphaned by me
Long-suffering, ferocious, stubborn, provident
Finch, bitch, ant, wild boar
Love letter with spelling mistakes
My mother: bread I sliced
Each day with her own knife.[6]

Josefina, or Pepita as she was known, was Paz's immediate connection to Spain and Europe. As with his appearance, this heritage set Paz apart from many other Mexicans, and questions of how 'Spanish' Mexicans are surfaces time and again in his work, especially in his magisterial *Sor Juana: Her Life and Her World*.[7] In his early twenties he rushed back to Spain to witness the Civil War and, after the defeat of the Republicans, welcomed many of the exiled writers in Mexico. At the same time, however, he stressed that to be born in America meant that he could also lay claim to a different tradition and approach to the world: much of his poetry and essays is devoted to exploring the dimensions of this difference.

In *Pasado en claro* Octavio Paz writes of families as being 'breeding-grounds for scorpions',[8] and yet the intensity of his descriptions of his own shows that family relationships are far more complex. Paz the poet is well aware that his personal beliefs and qualities owe a huge amount not only to what he inherited from the two sides of his family (the Mexican, indigenous roots on his paternal side, the Hispanic tradition that was the legacy of his mother and her ancestors), but also to the feelings of love and the longing for affection that arise from childhood. Throughout his work, male figures offer a challenge and a possible threat, while woman is there to provide reconciliation with the world through love, and to offer solace and warmth.

Almost as powerful as the presence and influence of his family on the young boy was the sense of place that the adult Paz recalls when looking back on his childhood.[9] The town of Mixcoac where Paz's grandfather took his family to live in 1915 was one of a series of pre-Hispanic settlements that ringed the capital but were still completely separate from it in the valley of Mexico. Until 1930 Mexico City had fewer than a million inhabitants; people living in the southern towns of Mixcoac, San Angel and Coyoacán talked of 'going to Mexico' when they boarded the trams that were their main link to the city. The streets of Mixcoac were cobbled with *tezontle*, the hard, purple-hued volcanic rock that originally formed the shores of the pre-discovery Tenochtitlán's lakes, and the town was still grouped around its central square, as it had been since the Spaniards conquered Mexico in the sixteenth century. The house and garden where Octavio Paz grew up, and where he was to live until his departure for the Yucatán and then Spain in 1937 at the

The town of Mixcoac, outside Mexico City, in the early 1920s.

Mixcoac town centre during Paz's childhood years.

age of 23, is portrayed by him in his later years as little short of a
Garden of Eden.[10] They appear throughout his poetry as the emo-
tional centre of his world, for example in a poem like 'La higuera'
in ¿Aguila o sol?,[11] and it is surely no coincidence that Paz's one
play, La hija de Rappaccini,[12] revolves around a young man gazing
out onto a garden and falling in love with the young woman
strolling there. At the same time, this paradise was under threat:
as Paz told Rita Guibert in 1970,[13] the years of revolution brought
grave economic problems to the family, and the Mixcoac house
soon fell into disrepair:

> Our house, full of antique furniture, books, and other objects,
> was gradually crumbling to bits. As rooms collapsed we moved
> the furniture into another. I remember that for a long time I
> lived in a spacious room with part of one of the walls missing.
> Some magnificent screens protected me inadequately from
> wind and rain. A creeper invaded my room . . .

The year 1920 saw Paz's father living in exile in the United States.[14]
When he sent for his wife and son to join him in Los Angeles, the boy

Octavio found himself in a strange world, where he was the outsider. This gave him an insight into the different customs and beliefs in two neighbouring societies that was to underpin much of his subsequent work, including his most famous analysis of Mexican identity, *El laberinto de la soledad*. As he recalled in old age:

> No sooner had we arrived than my parents decided I should go to the local kindergarten. I was six and didn't speak a word of English. I can vaguely remember my first day in class – the U.S. flag flying over the school building, the bare classroom with its desks and hard benches, my confused embarrassment at my classmates' noisy questioning, the gentle smile of the teacher trying to keep them in check. This was an Anglo-Saxon school – only two of all the other pupils were Mexican, and both of them had been born in Los Angeles. Terrified by my inability to understand what was going on, I took refuge in silence.[15]

This first uprooting did not last long. Within two years the family was back in Mixcoac with the grandfather and Aunt Amalia. Once again, according to his recollections in *Itinerary*, Octavio felt the outsider,[16] and it is at this point that he began to write, to explore his intense feelings in verse and prose. Looking back on this time in *Pasado en claro*,[17] he added a further source as the impulse to write: the death of his grandfather in 1924, when he was just ten years old: 'In death, I discovered language', he wrote.

Both his grandfather and his father were strongly anti-clerical republicans, but it appears to have been his Catholic mother who prevailed when it came to Paz's early education. He was enrolled first at the La Salle brothers' primary school in the former hacienda of El Zacatito in the centre of Mixcoac, and then at Williams College in southern Mexico City. At the latter, as Paz writes in *Itinerary*, he received a faithful copy of a true English public school education: 'They cultivated the body as a source of energy and fighting. It was an education destined to produce active, intelligent animals of prey. They worshipped manly values like tenacity, strength, loyalty and aggression.'[18] But the young boy's loyalty to his mother did not mean that he believed for long in her Catholic god. As Paz told Rita Guibert in 1970, he soon fought against the idea, and he claims that on one occasion when he felt no effect from taking communion, he spat on the ground, cursed God, and from then on decided he too would be 'belligerently' anti-religious.[19] From this point onwards, Paz's interest in religion seems to have been entirely intellectual. His early essays on poetry speak of the similarities between religious and poetic experience, but he always draws a clear distinction between them. And although the years spent in India and the Far East led him to explore Hinduism and Buddhism, this was as part of his investigations of different cultures and their expression in art rather than a search for a religious truth in which he could believe.

The closed world of the house and garden in Mixcoac suddenly expanded when, at the age of sixteen, the young Paz made the great leap from being educated locally to go daily to the centre of Mexico City for two years of 'prep' for entry into the national university. The classes took place at the San Ildefonso College, a former Jesuit seminary in a beautiful building in the heart of the old city, close to the main Zócalo square. These two years were crucial for Paz's development as both poet and polemicist. By the end of the 1920s, when Paz began attending the Preparatoria Nacional, the Mexican revolution was evolving into a new phase. The National Revolutionary Party (which in time became the Institutional Revolutionary Party, which was to hold power in Mexico for the next seventy years) sought to consolidate the gains of the revolution. Its leaders argued that what Mexico most needed after the years of political and economic turmoil was proper organization and a commitment to stability and peace. Others on the left felt the Mexican revolution had not gone far enough. They were clamouring for a proper 'socialist' society in the

A student orator at San Ildefonso College, Mexico City, late 1920s.

mould of Soviet Russia. For their part the Soviets considered Mexico as a country ripe for further change, and sent high-profile representatives as emissaries. The writer Alexandra Kollontai, for example, was its first ambassador when diplomatic relations were restored in 1927.[20] Octavio Paz may even have been one of the thousands of people who turned out to greet her on her arrival in the Mexican capital.

Above all, enthusiastic young Mexicans like Paz felt that the years of revolutionary violence in Mexico had catapulted their country into the modern era and onto the world stage. For almost the first time in Mexico's history, the people had become the protagonists of their own destiny, and this had linked them to what was happening in the post-revolutionary Soviet Union, and to the ideas of historical determinism espoused by Karl Marx and his followers. As Paz was to write later in *Itinerary*, 'My generation was the first in Mexico which lived world history as its own.'[21]

Paz's early political activism was channelled into one of the many cultural groups formed at San Ildefonso and the National University. At the age of sixteen he joined the grandly named Unión Estudiantil Pro-Obrero y Campesino (Union of Students, Workers and Peasants), set up in 1926 to offer education for the workers and help usher in the proletarian revolution. The adolescent Paz flung himself into debates about whether Mexico should adopt 'socialist education' as a means to creating a 'socialist society', according to the arguments of the great thinker and education minister José Vasconcelos,[22] or whether it was necessary to create a socialist society before the education system could become truly revolutionary. These arguments often spilled out onto the streets of the capital, where students and workers took on the police in protests against abuses of power by the Plutarco Calles government. When young Paz was briefly arrested briefly during a couple of these demonstrations, it was his lawyer father who secured his release.

Together with his political activity, Paz was already launching himself as a poet. The very first poem he published appeared in the Sunday supplement of *El Nacional* on 7 June 1931, when he was seventeen. It is entitled 'Juego' ('Game'):

Saquearé a las estaciones,
Jugaré con los meses y los años
(días de invierno con caras rojas de veranos).
Y por la senda gris,
Entre la muda procesión
De los días duros y inmóviles
Colocaré a los azules y gimnásticos.

I will put the seasons to the sword
Will play with months and years
(Winter days with their red summer faces).
And along the grey pathway
In among the silent procession
Of the harsh, unmoving days
I will place azure, gymnastic ones.[23]

There is no sign as yet of the political commitment that soon came to dominate his early works, although it is interesting to note that from the outset Paz the poet is determined to prove that he can change things, to shake up the old order in favour of something more vital and life-giving.

A further sign of his determination to pursue a literary career came soon afterwards, when the seventeen-year-old student got together with three friends to start his first literary review. This was called *Barandal* ('Handrail'), apparently named after the handrail of a cloister in San Ildefonso where the young students met to discuss politics and literature and generally to set the world to rights. The tone of the editorial in the first issue, published in September 1933 (though not written by Paz himself) could not be more eloquent:

> The intelligentsia in the USSR creates and constructs, and in capitalism copies and destroys. An intelligentsia which was and is a useless benefit in so many generations destroyed, exhausted, lost by the system . . . Just look at Marcel Proust! So intelligent, and yet someone who could only try to remember the past, who could not face the future . . .[24]

The first poems Octavio published in the magazine (which lasted for seven issues) and elsewhere show the influence of the older generation of Mexican poets such as Carlos Pellicer (their literature teacher at the college), Xavier Villaurrutia, and in general the group known as the *Contemporáneos* (Contemporaries), who published a review with the same title. As the name suggests, the *Contemporáneos* wanted to bring Mexican poetry up to date, to shake it out of the romantic lyricism it had been stuck in through the years of the revolution. These poets were determined to look outwards, to Europe, the United States or even Japan, for ways to express their feelings and experiences. The *Contemporáneos* movement was a rejection of any arrogant nationalism in literature, and at the same time a rejection of the 'machismo' associated with the masculine world of violence and struggle. The writers in the group also resisted any attempt to glorify the revolution, to make epics out of the years of fighting and the emergence of a new Mexico. They left this epic vision to muralist painters such as Diego Rivera, and in literature to the school of novelists emerging from the revolution.

These were the masters for the early Paz. They taught him to experiment, to play games with poetic form and yet at the same time to consider poetry as a deadly serious endeavour. Their magazine also put him in touch with what was new in poetry from around the world. However revolutionary his nascent political ideas may have been, it was two conservative voices that caught his attention: *Anabase* by the lofty French aristocrat Saint-John Perse or T. S. Eliot, whose impact he was to recall many years later: 'In the August 1930 issue of the magazine appeared a long and extraordinary poem which I read with astonishment, amazement and fascination: *The Waste Land*.'[25] This was the start of his distinction between what was innovative and new in poetry and the new and revolutionary in history: as he argued in *La otra voz*,[26] the temptation for many twentieth-century poets has been to consider the two as synonymous. As well as the *Contemporáneos*, Paz was an avid reader of the Spanish 'Generation of '27', which included poets such as Rafael Alberti, Federico García Lorca and Luis Cernuda – the latter soon to become a close friend and poetic mentor. He also discovered contemporary Latin American writing, and in particular Jorge Luis Borges, thanks to the important Argentine literary review *Sur*, to which Paz subsequently became a contributor.[27]

Equally important in view of Paz's later development was the almost simultaneous publication (in *Barandal*, December 1931) of his first reflection on the meaning and role of poetry in society: 'Etica del artista'. This is Paz's discussion of an age-old debate, a polemic made particularly relevant by the turbulent days Mexico and the rest of the world experienced in the early 1930s. What, the young poet asks himself, are the relative values of 'committed' (*arte de tésis*) as against 'pure' art (*arte puro*)? As he puts it:

To the former, the fundamental question is the almost religious intent of their work. Art as propaganda. As polemic. Art in the public arena. To the latter, the artist should simply be an artist. His work of art should be just that. With no other intent. Art is not play. Nor politics. Nor economy. Nor charity. It is art and nothing more.[28]

Somewhat surprisingly, considering his first poems and their ludic and experimental qualities, in this early essay Paz comes down on the side of 'committed' poetry. He concludes that young poets in America 'are part of a continent whose history it is up to us to make', and in consequence opts for artistic production that will contribute to helping build the future rather than concerning itself with attaining formal perfection.

Given his obvious devotion to literature at even this early age, a further contradiction was his decision to move on from San Ildefonso to the Faculty of Law at the University of Mexico in 1932. This appears to have been a concession to his father, but it was also a means of joining in the cultural activities of the most prominent centre of learning in the country. As well as offering him the opportunity to continue with his radical student activities, his studies also gave him time to write. A companion of his at the Faculty has spoken of how, as a student, Octavio always approached any new idea or argument as if it was the first time the matter had ever been thought about or discussed. He threw himself into every debate with total enthusiasm – another trait that was to remain with him all his life. The Law Faculty was far more traditional in atmosphere than San Ildefonso (with a strong Jesuit influence) but Paz was still closely involved in 'revolutionary' student politics. In 1934 he was sent as part of the UEPOC delegation to Veracruz on the Gulf of Mexico to study the situation of the workers there and to offer legal advice to people claiming land offered by the revolutionary authorities – a job his father had often done before him.

It was while studying at the university in 1934 that he met the first great love of his life, the woman who within a few years was to become his wife. Elena Garro was also a student, the daughter of a recent immigrant from Spain, José Antonio Garro. It was thanks to him that the young Octavio was first introduced to the world of the Orient, since José Antonio was a great reader of the Indian classics, from the *Bhaghavadgita* to the Upanishads and the work of Khrishnamurti, who at that time had a significant following in the West and visited Mexico around this time. Elena was a dancer and choreographer, with shining blonde hair that all her friends remarked on. The relationship between the two youngsters soon became so intense that her strict Catholic parents took measures to see that she was chaperoned whenever they met, and even threatened to remove her to a convent school. This threat only served to increase the young poet's passion: he wrote her page after page of wild letters: 'I don't want you to think of me with repulsion, as a sin,' he wrote in July 1935. 'We have to love our sins, because that is the only way we can be saved, by recognizing ourselves in them, and so ennobling ourselves.'[29]

The love-struck Paz continued to publish poetry. In 1932 the first poem appeared which he considered worth retaining in his later anthologies. This is 'Nocturno', and its scope and skilful construction show how far he has progressed formally and imaginatively in just one year. Once again, this early poem deals with a topic he was to return to again and again in his subsequent work: how can the poet find the exact words to describe the chaotic profusion of reality all around him? Is he doomed to mere solipsism as the words fail to capture the reality of a moment which has gone forever?

In the following year Paz published his first slim volume of poems: *Luna Silvestre* ('Wild Moon'). Only 75 copies of this 35-page pamphlet were produced, using offcuts from larger books printed by editor Miguel N. Lira.[30] The atmosphere of these poems is that of late romanticism: melancholy moonlight and even more melancholy love, woman as solace for misunderstood, passionate youth. Once again, the commitment to changing the world and making history that the young poet called for in his essay, as well as in his continuing political activities, is noticeably absent from the seven poems. It is hardly surprising that, still in his teens, his written work is inconsistent; the young poet was busy absorbing influences, studying the work of contemporaries and past masters, experimenting in order to find a voice of his own.

The next two years, from 1934 to 1936, were entirely taken up with studying, reading and his passionate relationship with Elena. He also found time to participate in another short-lived magazine, *Cuadernos del valle de México*. Then, on 8 March 1936 at the age of 52, his father was killed, apparently being hit by a train while wandering drunk on the tracks in the village of Los Reyes-La Paz, in Texcoco, just outside Mexico City. His remains were handed over to the family in a canvas sack. Many years later, the violence and senselessness of this death led Paz to write:

> *Por los durmientes y los rieles*
> *De una estación de moscas y de polvo*
> *Una tarde juntamos sus pedazos.*

> Among the sleepers and the rails
> Of a station of flies and dust
> One afternoon we gathered his bits.[31]

Apart from this reference, and a sequence in an uncollected poem written in 1939, Paz did not write about his father's death. Although it must have had a profound effect on him, at least as far as his poetry was concerned, at the time he was busy with other matters. This became plain a few months later, when the young writer published a poem that was radically different from his earlier offerings. The occasion for the new publication was the outbreak of the Spanish

Civil War in July 1936, when General Francisco Franco rebelled against the Republican government. Given not only his family ties with Spain but his ardent political convictions, Paz's sympathies were immediately with the loyalists. In September 1936 he published the pamphlet *¡No pasaran!* ('They Shall Not Pass!'),[32] which took up the battle cry made famous by the Communist leader in Spain Dolores Ibarruri (*La Pasiónaria*) during the desperate defence of Madrid in the months immediately following the military uprising. The poem was Paz's first success – it was printed in an edition of 3,500 copies, with all proceeds given to the Spanish Popular Front in Mexico. Here, finally, the 22-year-old found a convincing vehicle for his 'committed' poetry. Written in a few weeks over the summer of 1936, the poem shows a real spontaneity of feeling, and an immediate identification with what he saw as a noble and revolutionary cause. It is public pamphleteering, and there are many empty rhetorical phrases in the poem's six pages, but the sentiments are genuine, and the poem is at least partially successful in fulfilling the fledgling poet's wish to create a work that engages directly with political reality. It is also the first of his poems obviously written to be declaimed out loud to an audience. As such, it stresses a simple opposition between the life-giving Republic and the deadly, paralysing effects of Franco and his followers:

> *Detened a la muerte.*
> *A esos muros siniestros, sanguinarios,*
> *oponed otros muros;*
> *reconquistad la vida detenida,*
> *el correr de los ríos paralizados*
> *el crecer de los campos prisioneros,*
> *reconquistad a España de la muerte.*

> Bring death to a halt.
> Against those sinister, bloodthirsty walls

Build other walls;
Reconquer halted life,
The flow of paralysed rivers
The growth of imprisoned fields,
Reconquer Spain from death.[33]

But while *¡No pasarán!* confirmed that Paz had found the possibility for political and social involvement which he himself had declared indispensable for poetry, his next published work marked a return to more personal concerns. In January 1937 *Raíz del hombre* ('Root of Man') appeared, once again in a much smaller edition of 600 copies, published in Mexico City by Simbad editions.[34] The cantos of this first edition (later editions saw the length greatly reduced) combine to create one long erotic musing. This is the earliest example of Paz's use of the long poem, a form he had admired in Eliot and St-John Perse, and to which he returned in his essay on the poetic voice, 'La otra voz', towards the end of his life.[35] Here the extended form allows him to suggest the effects of time, the possibility of reflection on experience, the pulsation of life in movement. It is plain that some of the poets he has been reading are the German Romantics – the epigraph is from Goethe, and the spirit of the poem is close to Novalis, but critics have also noted a close similarity with the work of D. H. Lawrence, and in particular *Lady Chatterley's Lover* (which Paz had read in 1934). The English novelist (Paz was apparently not yet aware of his poetry) offered the Mexican writer an example of the exultant celebration of physical love.

In *Raíz del hombre* the woman desired is no longer a distant goddess figure as in his adolescent poems. Now she has become a life force, while passion is a purifying torrent that sweeps everything away, sets everything ablaze, and offers the possibility of transcendence. Striking images lead the reader through the poet's search for woman and the triumphal moment of union, which is immediately followed by a seemingly inevitable separation. This gives rise to a sense of complete despair, only resolved by the end of the poem thanks to an acceptance that this is the dual nature of love: the supreme moment which annuls the passage of time, followed by a reluctant re-insertion into the normal flow of temporal existence. In his introduction to a volume of this early work published in 1993 (*Primera Instancia: Poesía 1930–1943*) Paz, at least in hindsight, saw the poem as part of his general belief system at the time:

> I had elaborated a sort of vague theory of sexuality in which the carnal embrace was an instant and miniature representation of the cosmic process. Like the suns and the planets, when men and women embrace they fall into infinite space. This fall is a return to the origin, the beginning, but also, after several eons or several moments, a resurrection.[36]

The year 1937 was the first great watershed in Paz's life. Following his father's death, he finally decided to abandon the legal career towards which his university studies were meant to be leading him. To help his mother financially he started going out to work, taking on jobs as a typist in the National Archive and as a speechwriter for a revolutionary politician. A few months later, he also left his childhood home in Mixcoac, initially to spend several months in the remote southern region of the Yucatán and then, in quick succession, to marry Elena Garro and to set off on his first trip to Europe.

In Europe, Paz was immediately confronted not only with the horrors of the civil war in Spain, but with writers who were more than willing to sacrifice principles to preserve their ideological 'purity'. His previous hope that revolution, the desire for freedom and poetry could go smoothly hand-in-hand was rapidly demolished. Experiences in Spain were to shape his political belief in a rational, critical liberalism that was to remain with him for the rest of his life.

2

Taking a Stand, 1937–43

In March 1937 the aeroplane taking the 22-year-old poet from Mexico City to the distant city of Mérida in the Yucatán peninsula took two days to complete its journey. The Yucatán had always been one of the most isolated regions of Mexico, closer in spirit, geography and population to the countries of Central America. In the nineteenth century, when Mexico won its freedom from Spain, the Yucatán declared its own independence, and was only reincorporated into the federal state in 1848. It was not until a century later that the peninsula was properly linked to the capital by railway and roads; even in the 1930s rich families often sent their children off by sea to Cuba, Spain or France to be educated rather than to the remote Mexican capital.

But 1930s Yucatán was one of the regions where the inequalities of life in Mexico were most evident. In the early years of the twentieth century, its capital Mérida was reputed to have more millionaires per head of population than anywhere else in the Americas. This was thanks to the boom in demand in Europe for sisal, the rope made from the henequen plant that grew on the haciendas, the vast agricultural properties situated in the otherwise barren landscape of the peninsula. It was here too that the local indigenous population, descendants of the Maya who had built the great pyramids and other ritual centres in the region, were still being employed in near-slave conditions. In the second half of the 1930s, the federal government of Lázaro Cárdenas began to expropriate the haciendas, and to try to

Straw-roofed hut, Yucatán: 1930s poverty in the Mexican countryside.

improve working conditions for the peasant farmers. As part of this effort, the federal ministry of education wanted to set up schools for the sons and daughters of the working population, most of whom had no schooling at all, and spoke only Mayan languages rather than Spanish. This was the mission that Octavio Paz and his colleagues were charged with in Mérida. Too young officially to be named director of the school that the secretary of education had funded, he helped set it up, recruit pupils and, when term started in April 1937, began to teach 'Hispanic literature'.[1] Almost as soon as he arrived, Paz began to write regularly for a local newspaper, and set up a 'Pro-Democracia Española' committee. Deeply affected by the poverty of the rural *mestizo* majority, as well as by the stark white limestone landscape, he wrote a series of articles or *Notas* on his first impressions of the region,[2] and also began to collect material for a book of poetry. This was *Entre la piedra y la flor* ('Between Stone and Flower'), eventually published in 1941.[3]

Paz's first foray outside Mexico City lasted only a few months. It ended when he embarked on a much longer journey in June 1937. This took him both to war-torn Spain and to a first stay in Paris, where the France imagined from his grandfather's library, his aunt's French lessons and the translations read in Mexican magazines, at last became a reality. The European journey began when the young poet received an invitation to travel to Spain as part of the Mexican delegation to the Second International Congress of Antifascist Writers, a symposium of left-wing intellectuals backed by the Spanish Republican government. A previous Congress had been held in Paris in 1935; now more than one hundred delegates from thirty different countries were invited to the second one, held in Republican Spain to show international support for their cause. In his autobiography, *Confieso que he vivido* (translated as 'Memoirs'), the Chilean poet Pablo Neruda, appointed one of the Congress organizers in Paris, gives himself the credit for Paz's inclusion in the Mexican delegation: 'I felt in some way proud to have brought him. He had only published one book, which I had received two months earlier and which seemed to me to contain a real seed. Nobody knew him in those days.'[4] Despite this generous gesture, during the Congress Paz became horrified at Neruda's intransigent political stance, and soon after-wards, back in Mexico, the two men were to have a public falling-out that led to their estrangement for many years.

So Paz left Mérida and the Yucatán after little more than three months, never to return to his teaching post. But there was one more thing he had to do before leaving for Spain. This was to marry his great love Elena Garro, whose parents would not dream of her accompanying the impetuous young poet to Europe until their rela-tionship was properly sealed. The couple were married in a civil ceremony in Mexico City at the end of May 1937: Paz was twenty-three, his bride not yet eighteen. They presented their marriage as a *fait accompli* to their parents, and went to live with Paz's mother in Mixcoac before setting out for Spain. Paz was joined on the long trip to Europe by another invited poet, Carlos Pellicer, a left-wing Catholic from the earlier generation of the *Contemporáneos* group. The two men and Elena Garro travelled by car from Mexico City to

New York, but had to continue on to Canada to find a transatlantic liner to take them across the Atlantic to France. The LEAR (Liga de Escritores y Artistas Revolucionarios), which saw itself as the official representative of Mexican revolutionary culture (in other words, following the official Communist Party line) were concerned that Mexico was to be represented by a Catholic (Pellicer) and someone who had never been a party member (Paz). They soon dispatched one of their loyal members, the journalist and essayist José Mancisidor, to join the other two to represent Mexico in Spain.[5] As Paz recalled during a meeting of exiled Spanish Republicans in Paris commemorating the fifteenth anniversary of the 19 July uprising, his position was clearcut: 'All you had to do was open your eyes: on the one hand, the old world of violence and lies, with its symbols – Helmet, Cross, Umbrella; on the other, the face of a man, so real it was like an hallucination, with bare chest and no party insignia.'[6]

In Paris, Paz and his companions were enthusiastically welcomed by the French Communist poet Louis Aragon, and by Pablo Neruda. It was during this short stay in the French capital that the young Mexican first met the Peruvian poet César Vallejo, already in his final illness, as well as the Spanish film-maker Luis Buñuel, who was later to become a close friend during his exile in Mexico. The Mexican party joined André Malraux, Ilya Ehrenburg and the English poet Stephen Spender (who seems to have been struck mostly by the Paz couple's extreme youth and beauty) on the long train journey down to the Spanish port city of Valencia, to where the Spanish Republican government had recently moved because of the bitter siege of Madrid by Franco's forces.

The second Congress of intellectuals was held in three cities still in Republican hands: Valencia, Madrid and Barcelona, with final sessions back in Paris. The agenda included debates on the role of the writer in revolutionary society, the social responsibility of the writer and many other topics, and was intended to show support for the Spanish Republic by demonstrating the vitality of left-wing thought.

Many of the most prominent left-wing writers and intellectuals from Western Europe had rallied to the call, whilst among the other Latin Americans whom Paz met were the composer Silvestre Revueltas, David Siquieros, Alejo Carpentier and Vicente Huidobro. However, the debates at the Congress soon degenerated into efforts to get the delegates to publicly repudiate the French writer André Gide. A member of the French Communist Party, and one of France's best-known and influential writers, Gide, who had presided at the 1935 Paris Congress, had fallen foul of his comrades because of a book he had published on his return from a long stay in the Soviet Union: *Retour de l'urss* (1936). His crime, according to many of the intellectuals at the congress, was not merely to have criticized aspects of life in the Soviet Union, but to have suggested that they were endemic to the revolution rather than transitional problems. The Communists at the Congress argued that any criticism of the Soviet revolution was playing directly into the hands of the Fascists. In what was to become a much-repeated argument, they called for uncritical support of the Soviet Union and its great leader Josef Stalin in order to present a united front against the common enemy.

Paz wrote of his attitude towards the Gide affair:

The Latin American delegations held several private sessions, in which Gide's book was discussed, his attitude and the need to repudiate him. There was a proposal to draw up a condemnation signed by all the Latin American delegates, and there was a vote to try and make the decision unanimous. Carlos Pellicer defended Gide's right to think differently and to express his opinions openly. In the final vote over the condemnation of Gide, there were only two abstentions: Pellicer's and mine. In the end, the condemnation was never drawn up, because in that evening's public session, José Bergamín launched such a virulent attack on Gide that the delegates decided it was unnecessary.[7]

According to Paz in later life, the Congress was the moment when the scales fell from his eyes, when he saw how pernicious it was for writers and intellectuals to subordinate their art to the dictates of a political party. He was also horrified at the personal nature of the attacks: he himself could be passionate and critical in argument, but always tried to debate principles and ideals rather than involve personalities. As one of the youngest writers at the Congress, he did not get much chance to present his views in the main forums, which lasted from 4 to 12 July 1937. During that week, Paz, Elena Garro and many other Congress delegates were taken to Madrid, still encircled by Franco's forces. This was the first opportunity Paz had to see the war at first hand and, according to his wife, he reacted with typical enthusiasm:

> We went down to the Paseo de Rosales in a very relaxed mood. There we ran into a gun battle. I ran for the trench, and the others followed. 'Now they'll mortar us,' I said. Carlos Pellicer was livid, but Paz said: 'This is magnificent!' We ran along the trench and out the far end of it, still running for our lives under a hail of bullets, until we reached a street that was perpendicular to the Paseo. 'I've damaged my liver. I'll never listen to you heroic children again,' Pellicer complained. I thought – we've seen a tiny bit of the war, and isn't that why we came?[8]

But in addition to this enjoyment of the excitement of warfare, the young poet was also storing up the experience in order to make poetry out of it. What he saw in the streets of Madrid that week surfaced in one of his major poems of the 1950s, *Piedra de Sol* ('Sunstone'), where it has become an occasion for the re-affirmation of life in the midst of death and destruction:

> *Madrid, 1937,*
> *En la plaza del Angel las mujeres*
> *Cosían y cantaban con sus hijos,*

Después sonó la alarma y hubo gritos,
Casas arrodilladas en el polvo,
Torres hendidas, frentes escupidas
Y el huracán de los motores, fijo:
Los dos se desnudaron y se amaron
Por defender nuestra porción eterna,
Nuestra ración de tiempo y paraíso
Tocar nuestra raíz y recobrarnos,
Recobrar nuestra herencia arrebatada
Por ladrones de vida hace mil siglos . . .

Madrid, 1937,
In the plaza del Angel women
Were sewing and singing with their children
Then the alarm sounded and there were shouts,
Houses brought to their knees in the dust,
Towers torn apart, facades spat out
And the unmoving hurricane of engines:
The two of them stripped naked and made love
To defend our share of eternity
Our ration of time and paradise
To reach our root and regain ourselves,
Regain our inheritance stolen
By the thieves of life a thousand centuries ago . . .[9]

The Congress itself limped to a conclusion in Barcelona, with
the closing sessions held in Paris on the weekend of 16–17 July.
Once again most of the delegates' energy was spent on further attacks
on Gide, as well as a final resolution in which the 'cultural workers'
resolved to fight Fascism 'by whatever means' and reaffirmed their
'unshakeable confidence in the triumph of the Spanish people'. It
was left to the President of the Spanish Republic, Manuel Azaña, to
sum up the whole sorry experience in his diary: 'The Congress was

useless. Few people came, and very few of any weight . . . It cost the state a fortune, and yet on the day of the first session there were no typewriters, no paper, no stenographers.'[10]

Paz did not go back to Paris for the closure of the Congress, preferring to stay on in Valencia for several weeks. This was particularly because he had become friendly with the young writers associated with the influential magazine *Hora de España*, including Manuel Altolaguirre, Juan Gil-Albert, Antonio Sánchez-Barbudo, María Zambrano and Luis Cernuda, another poet who was later to become a close friend. Despite the Communist attempts to control culture in Republican Spain, the members of the magazine insisted that although they accepted the social responsibility of literature, they would not be bound by any party line. They wanted socially responsible poetry but also complete freedom in regard to their own art. This was precisely Paz's position. Although still convinced that Marxist revolution represented the best hope for the regeneration of society in both Mexico and Europe, he never wanted his poetry to express a direct political message. While he rejected the stance of poets such as Juan Ramón Jiménez (who had already left Spain for exile, and whom Paz met in Cuba during a stopover on his return journey to Mexico) who argued that poetry represented values and ideals opposed to those of ideology and the everyday political struggle, and could only suffer by concerning itself with them, Paz could never accept that propaganda as such could produce good poetry. This remained his attitude throughout his life: in a 1994 interview, for example, he defended his earlier, more explicit poetry in these terms: 'my political poems never obeyed the dictates of the Party, and I don't consider them as propaganda. I wrote them out of the same impulse that leads me to write love poems, poems about trees, or any state of mind. They all express my human condition.'[11]

It was thanks to the members of *Hora de España* that in 1937 Paz brought out his third published book of poems, *Bajo tu clara sombra y otros poemas sobre España* ('In Your Clear Shade and other

Poems about Spain').[12] This volume makes a clear distinction between his passionate love poetry and his poetry of social protest, but as Juan Gil-Albert emphasized in his review for the magazine: 'when a young man writes these poems in which life shines out, he is, for the mere fact of having written them, on the side of the revolution that men desire'.[13] At the same time, it is clear that by now Paz had given up the hope of his father's generation that the Mexican Revolution could provide the answer to the building of a more just and fulfilling society in his home country. This pessimism is reflected in a lecture on contemporary Mexican poetry to the Valencia Atheneum in August 1937, when Paz told his audience: 'If the generation prior to ours wished for and got men who were broken, unfortunate and cruelly fragmented, we live in hope of a mankind who can be reborn, in a revolutionary way, from his own ashes, reborn more intensely alive, more lucidly anguished.'[14]

The tone here is far removed from any optimistic belief that the Marxist revolution is just around the corner, in Mexico or in Spain. Poetry for Paz is already seen as upholding spiritual and moral rather than directly political values; it strengthens a sense of common humanity rather than directly supporting the political struggle dominated by party affiliations and loyalties. In consequence, it was the shared experiences with others that most affected him during these months in Spain. One incident which stuck in the young poet's mind sufficiently for him to recall it in interview more than thirty years later was when he found himself caught up in a Fascist bombardment in a village on the outskirts of Valencia:

We went through it singing the 'Internationale' to keep up our own courage and also to encourage the inhabitants, and then we took shelter in a vegetable garden. The peasants came to look at us, and were interested to hear I was a Mexican. Mexico was sending help to the Republicans, and some of those peasants were anarchists. They went back to their houses in the middle of the bombardment to look for food, and brought us a little bread, a melon, cheese and wine. Eating with those peasants during a bombardment . . . that's something I can't forget.[15]

This sense of solidarity did, however, lead to at least a fleeting desire to play a more direct role in the war. At some point over the summer of 1937 Paz's enthusiasm for the cause appears to have led him to wish to join the fight to defend the Republic as a political commissar. This reflects a naïve conviction that his enthusiasm and talents would immediately make him the ideal recruit: the reality was that by this stage in the war, it was the Communist Party that controlled all appointments of this kind. It would only name trusted party members to such sensitive positions, as Paz later realized:

I got the idea I should join the army as a political commissar – that was an aberration. I made some enquiries, but was put out by the way I was received; I was told I had no experience, and that above all I was lacking the most important thing: the backing of a political party or a revolutionary organization. I was a man without a party, nothing more than a sympathizer, so someone in authority told me very sensibly 'you can be more useful with a typewriter than with a machine-gun'.[16]

Once the dream of picking up a rifle and fighting for the Republican cause had vanished, Paz and Elena Garro had to think how best they could support the Spanish loyalists. After several weeks in Valencia they moved on to Barcelona, and then in October 1937 travelled north to Paris, apparently hoping to secure visas to visit the Soviet Union. While waiting for these visas, Paz again met Alejo Carpentier, César Vallejo and the Spanish poet Miguel Hernández, who was on his way to the Soviet Union to attend a theatre festival on behalf of the Spanish Republican government. As a poet, Paz admired Hernández's use of popular ballad forms, which he felt showed he was genuinely in touch with the poorest country peasants of Spain. His first meeting made a huge impression on him, as he later told the French writer Claire Cea: 'The first time I saw Miguel, the Spanish poet was singing some popular songs. He had a raw bass voice, like that of an innocent animal. A rustic accent, a deep voice like an echo in a valley or a rock falling into a ravine.'[17] As a man, Paz admired the Spanish poet's courage and steadfast support for the Republican cause beyond all political infighting. After Hernández' death in a Francoist jail in 1942, he wrote a sombre epitaph: 'He died alone, in a hostile Spain, one that was an enemy of the Spain he spent his youth in, the adversary of the Spain his generosity dreamed of. Let others curse his executioners; let others analyse and study his poetry. I simply want to honour his name.'[18]

The young Mexican couple never succeeded in reaching the Soviet Union, and after six months in Europe, they returned to Mexico at the end of 1937. On the way back, Paz wrote an eloquent farewell to Spain and its war in the poem 'El barco' (later renamed 'Los Viejos'), apparently written when his ship crossed with that of another carrying refugees fleeing defeated Spain. Despite this bitterness, the 1941 version of the poem ends with the promise that their sacrifice can at least bring about the poet's salvation:

Allí los reconozco
Allí los nombro
Con los ardientes nombres de mis lagrimas
Y me disuelvo en ellos
Y me salvo.

There I recognize them
There I name them
With the burning names of my tears
I dissolve in them
And I am saved.[19]

Back in Mexico, Paz continued to try to drum up support for the Spanish cause, giving talks, organizing events and writing articles in support of the Republic. In July 1938, to commemorate the second anniversary of the struggle against Franco, he published an anthology – the first he had ever edited – of the work of nine loyal Spanish poets, spanning three generations. In the introduction, he repeated his belief that poetry was the deepest, most meaningful means of expression that a people had, ending with the claim that 'Spain speaks to us now, as it once again discovers in the voices of its poets, in the midst of tragedy and injustice, the lively, most loving communication with its people'. In spite of all the political chicanery he had been a witness to in Spain, throughout his life Paz continued to believe that the Spanish people's response to the Franco uprising in July 1936 was a glorious example of man's spontaneous desire for liberty. This notion of rebellion in the name of freedom also mirrored for him the way that poetry itself was born, as a rejection of the strictures and compromises imposed by everyday life, when it loses sight of the essential needs of mankind for liberty and love. The judgement he expressed to a meeting in support of the Spanish Republic held in Paris in July 1951 was typical:

What happened in Spain on 19 July 1936 was something that has never been seen since in Europe. The people, with no leaders, representatives, or intermediaries, took power . . . The spontaneity of this revolutionary action, the natural way in which the people assumed its role as leader during those days, and the effectiveness of its struggle, clearly showed the failings of those ideologies which claim to lead and direct a revolution.[20]

In that same year, 1938, Paz began to contribute to and later to edit the most influential literary magazine of the period in Mexico: *Taller de poesía*. In an editorial for the second issue, probably penned by him, the magazine editors established their distance from the

earlier *Contemporáneos* group, insisting that poetry had to look outwards to take in what was happening in everyday life around it, in
order to offer not only consolation but solidarity. At the same time,
as with *Hora de España*, the *Taller* group refused to toe any political
party line, and insisted on an open approach to political questions.
According to Paz, poetry was to be seen as part of lived experience,
the highest point of which implied a communion with the world that
could be best realised in moments of love. 'Love, like poetry was an
attempt to recover man from scission and rupture.'[21]

By 1939, many of the writers Paz had met in Spain as part of the
Hora de España group found themselves (often thanks to Paz's own
efforts) living in exile in Mexico, Gil-Albert and María Zambrano
among them. He repaid their support for him in Spain by welcom-
ing the exiles into the pages of the magazine, which by the end of
the decade became the most complete expression of Hispanic writing from the two continents. However, not everyone in Mexico was
so pleased with the increasing numbers of Spanish writers and
intellectuals who flooded to Mexico after the final defeat of the
Spanish Republic. The narrow-minded nationalist reaction this
influx caused in Mexican literary circles – *Taller* was attacked for
giving too much space to the newcomers, to the detriment of
Mexican authors – helped exacerbate a crisis in Paz's life. This crisis
was on many levels. On one level, he quickly became exhausted
with fighting this kind of blinkered nationalism. On another, he
was struggling with his political beliefs that a Marxist revolution
in Mexico, Spain and elsewhere could help mankind progress
towards a new level of solidarity.

At the same time, his poetry was undergoing a painful transition.
Until now, it had rested on two pillars: an impersonal social voice
that was now being undermined by his doubts over the possibility of
revolution, and intense love poems, which he was having to redefine
in the light of his growing realization of the gap between love as an
absolute and the lived reality of its inconstancy. By now in his late

twenties, Paz was also facing great economic difficulties. He had never finished a university degree, and so could not hope to pursue an academic career. He had no legal qualifications, and no taste for the profession. As a result he found himself having to do the kind of absurd jobs that struggling writers often have to do in any country. Thanks to a friend he was given an inspector's job in the Mexican banking system. One of his main tasks was to supervise the counting and burning of used banknotes – so every month, as he later wryly commented, millions of pesos passed through his hands, but they were of no use to him. He was also still employed by the Secretary of Education to give talks to primary school teachers, but never seems to have felt drawn to returning to teaching himself. Another of the jobs he found himself in was as a screenwriter for the burgeoning Mexican film industry. He even tried his hand at songwriting, penning the following lines for Jorge Negrete, the 1940s moustachioed Mexican heart-throb, in a film called *El Rebelde* (The Rebel):

Yo te miro con los ojos
Cuando los cierro te miro
Y en mi pecho te aprisiono
Con cerrojos de suspiro

I gaze at you
Even when I close my eyes
In my breast I imprison you
With the locks of my sighs[22]

Paz found perhaps more politically correct employment with the newspaper *El Popular*, published by the government-backed trade union, the Confederación de Trabajadores Mexicanos. He contributed news articles as well as cultural reports and opinion columns. In August 1939, the newspaper followed the orthodox Communist line of supporting the non-aggression pact signed between Germany and the Soviet Union. Paz could not agree, and for him the newspaper's position once again underlined the dangers of submitting to the dictates of a political party. He soon ceased to collaborate, although he did continue to write for literary magazines and the weekly *Novedades*, where some of his articles on life in Mexico were the germ of his *El laberinto de la soledad*, published at the end of the decade. He also encouraged his wife Elena Garro to take up a career in journalism, after the birth of their first and only child, Laura Helena Paz Garro, in December 1939. (See the poem 'Niña' written in her honour.[23]) The three of them lived in an apartment in the centre of Mexico City, which was a focus point for many of the young Mexican and exiled Spanish writers living in the capital.

In 1941 another collection of poems, *Entre la piedra y la flor* ('Between Stone and Flower'), appeared.[24] This extended sequence was mostly written during the months spent in the Yucatán four years earlier and, as with much of his early work, by the time it was published, the volume reflected ideas and values that Paz had already left behind. This first edition of *Entre la piedra y la flor* is a Marxist denunciation of the exploitation of the workers on the henequen plantations (it was republished in the 1970s in a much revised version, as by then Paz rejected what came to seem to him as a too-obvious political message). The work of the peasants is closely identified with the poet and his task, as both are seen to be denied value by the capitalist world. In the first section of the poem, as the title suggests, the life of the peasant is situated between the harsh stony land and the flower of the henequen plant, magnificent, sexual, but which only blooms once in the plant's lifespan. The second part of the poem focuses more on the poet and his reaction to the harshness all around him, the feelings of empathy and anger this creates. The third section looks at how the plant becomes a commodity, and is part of the unjust capitalist system, found at its most 'savage' in places such as the Yucatán, while the ending returns to a criticism of the capitalist system, contrasted with the life-enhancing values of peasant traditions and attitudes. In his note on the collection in the *Collected Works*, Paz described his intention in writing the book as 'to show the relation that, like a real strangler's knot, ties the concrete life of the peasants to the impersonal, abstract structure of the capitalist economy'.[25]

> El henequén,
> verde lección de geometria
> sobre la tierra blanca y ocre
> Agricultura, comercio, industria, lenguaje.
> Es una planta vivaz y es una fibra,
> es una acción en la bolsa y es un signo.
> Es tiempo humano,
> tiempo que se acumula,
> tiempo que se dilapida.

> Henequen
> Green lesson in geometry
> On the white and ochre land
> Agriculture, commerce, industry, language.
> It's a spiky plant and a fibre
> It's a share on the exchange and a sign.
> It's human time,
> Time accumulating,
> Time crumbling.[26]

The poem ends with a wish to 'para acabar con todo/ oh mundo seco/ para acabar con todo' ('bring it all to an end') but in general the work is not as strident as his Spanish social poetry. This is probably due to the fact that it was based on more direct observation, as Paz's poetry often proceeds out of a concrete situation that leads him to more philosophical reflections. The volume was not widely reviewed, but one critic (José Luis Martínez) praised it:

Henequen plantation, Yucatán, early 1930s.

'This book shows Mexico not as the picturesque or revolutionary commonplace, but the eternity and the harshness of its destiny.'[27]

By the time *Entre la piedra y la flor* was published, Paz no longer believed in the possibility of a liberating revolution in his own country. The hopeful years of the early 1930s under Lázaro Cárdenas had given way to an 'institutionalization' of the revolution and the building of power structures that were to last for a further sixty years. The chances that Republican Spain could blossom into a revolutionary society had been crushed forever by Franco's Fascism. France and other European liberal democracies were also threatened by the forces of Fascism. Nor could the regime built in the post-revolutionary Soviet Union offer the answers for Paz's search for a society built on solidarity. Despite all this, at this time Octavio Paz continued to believe in Marxism as offering the political way forward. This attitude appears to have been what led him to shun the French Surrealist leader André Breton when he came to visit the Soviet dissident revolutionary Leon Trotsky, who had been granted exile in Mexico in 1937. Since the early 1930s Breton had been insisting that there must be an alternative on the left to rigid Marxism dictated by the Soviet Communist Party. This had led to Surrealism splitting as a group, with Aragon and others preferring to put the political struggle – as defined by the French Communist party – as a more important priority than the 'Surrealist Revolution'. By the end of the decade, Breton was becoming increasingly isolated in France, and Surrealism's irreverent independent spirit was seen, not just by the Communists, as a refusal to commit to the fight for freedom. 'Breton was a notorious Trotskyist, and the name of Trotsky was anathema to us.'[28] But it was another decade before Paz came under the political and literary influence of Surrealism. In 1940 he wrote, in reply to a survey of attitudes towards the movement by the magazine *Romance*, 'Surrealism has done little more than to continue what Romanticism began; now, abandoned by the moderating muses – the muses of language – it has fallen into literature; in other words, into a language of clichés'.[29]

Soon afterwards, another polemical literary figure crossed Paz's path again. This was Pablo Neruda, who in 1941 was appointed the consul-general for Chile in Mexico. At first Paz apparently enjoyed the flamboyant parties the Chilean held, but the two were soon to fall out. The argument arose from *Laurel*, another anthology that Paz was editing, this time of modern poetry in the Spanish language, with his Spanish friends from *Hora de España* now living in Mexico. Both Neruda and the exiled Spanish poet León Felipe refused to appear in the book because they did not agree with the political persuasions of other poets included, and in the end Paz himself was not published there. Some time later, there was a drunken incident when

Neruda and Paz traded insults and almost came to blows. When Neruda left Mexico in 1943, Paz concluded: 'His literature is contaminated by politics, his politics by literature, and his criticism is often no more than friendly complicity. The result is it's hard to say who is talking: the official or the poet, the friend or the politician . . .'.[30] The two men only became reconciled in the late 1960s in London, but although Paz was always suspicious of the Chilean poet's continuing support for Communism, he saw him as a real poet, especially in his earlier collections such as *Residencia en la tierra*, before the bombast and grandiloquence took over.

Paz himself was extremely active as a poet during these years: *A la orilla del mundo*, a considerable book of some 150 pages, appeared in August 1942.[31] The volume included much of the poetry that had previously been published in small editions, plus some new poems. These stress above all the solitary nature of the poet's task. The poet must explore his inner world to try to find the moment of epiphany that can redeem the wasteful effects of ordinary time. Shortly afterwards, Paz became involved in another important magazine, *El Hijo pródigo*. In many ways, this was a continuation of *Taller*; its articles looked resolutely outwards from Mexico, and included many translations of important works originally in English or French. The magazine was also opposed to all political control of artistic expression: by now for Paz the watchword was 'lucid criticism'. Paz is thought to have written the magazine's editorials, including that of issue number 5 (August 1943): 'The writer, the poet, the artist, are not instruments, and their work can never be the blind missile that many people see it as. The only way to defeat Hitler and everything he signifies in terms of universal evil is to restore the freedom to criticize and denounce in the field of culture . . .'.[32]

It was in *El Hijo pródigo* that Paz published his up-to-date evaluation of what he saw as the possibilities of poetry in a disintegrating world. The occasion for the text was exiled poet José Bergamín's organization of a series of lectures to commemorate the four hundredth anniversary of the birth of the mystical poet San Juan de la Cruz. In his essay 'Poesía de soledad y poesía de comunión' ('Poetry of Solitude and Poetry of Communion') Paz argues that poetry's approach to the world is similar to that of religion, but that poetry can never accept authority, and must always be 'dissident'.[33] He goes on to compare and contrast the sixteenth-century world of Saint John of the Cross, which he sees as harmonious and of a piece with that of the seventeenth-century poet Quevedo. He sees the latter's situation as much closer to that of the contemporary writer, engaged in a basically solitary search for meaning in a world that has no place for him and places little value on his efforts. Although he mentions Marx as the 'most profound thinker' in modern history, Paz concludes that poetic revolt is of a different nature from political revolution, however scientific the basis for the latter might be. The essay concludes with a blistering list of false poetic prophets, including 'erotomaniacs who confuse their unhappiness with love', the 'pedantic hunchbacks', 'mystical onanists', as well as 'neo-catholics' and 'nationalist parrots', and 'criminals who think they are revolutionary simply because they shout and get drunk': in this way the frustrated young poet delivers his verdict on the poisonous atmosphere in the Mexican literary world as the Second World War was raging.

By the second half of 1943, with his thirtieth birthday fast approaching, it became plain that Paz needed to get out of the situation in which he found himself in Mexico. As well as the political and literary arguments and disappointments, he was still struggling to make ends meet, and his relationship with his wife was already rocky. A 1943 poem 'El Desconocido' ('The Stranger') hints at this disenchantment: 'en su boca la granada sangrienta de otra boca se hizo amargura, yel' ('In his mouth, the bloody pomegranate of another mouth tasted like bitter gall').[34] In order to escape this barrage of problems and uncertainties, Paz, still officially enrolled as a student, applied for a Guggenheim grant to go to the

United States and study 'America and its poetic expression'. In November 1943 he set off for California in a Greyhound bus without his wife and daughter. Although he lived in the United States for less than two years, it was to be almost a decade before he returned to Mexico. The period he spent away from his home country helped him produce his most celebrated book (*El laberinto de la soledad*),[35] and much of his most poignant poetry. In his short auto-biographical sketch *Itinerary* he describes what for him were the most important lessons he learnt in the United States:

> In the United States I experienced days of exhilaration and others of great depression. I read American and English poets tirelessly, and thanks to their example I started to write poems in Spanish free of the rhetoric that was still asphyxiating the young poets of Spain and Latin America. In a word, I felt reborn. I had never felt so alive. The war was on, and the American people was living through one of the greatest moments of its history. In Spain I had encountered fraternity in the face of death; in the United States I discovered the warmth of life.[36]

3

New Departures, 1943–53

In 1943 Paz was keen to leave all his personal problems and the literary disputes of Mexico behind him. This period in the US, his first prolonged stay outside Mexico on the American continent, was to provide him with an invaluable viewpoint from which he could observe his own country and the characteristics of his fellow countrymen in the mid-twentieth century. The tensions of Paz's life were also reflected in his poetry, where he was still trying to find convincing ways of incorporating his moral concerns in a way that would engage with the world around him without compromising his integrity. Formally, he was searching for new and simpler ways to express emotions and thoughts that were not straitjacketed by the rhetoric of the Spanish tradition. It is plain in these years that although he is convinced of the value of poetry, he is not as yet sure of his own voice or poetic worth. He himself wrote of his departure from Mexico as a search: 'A search for who or what? A search for Mexico or for myself, perhaps for a place in Mexico: my place. Or the place Mexico occupied in me. My wandering began with a feeling of strangeness and a question: am I the foreigner? Or is this land I call my own a foreign country?'[1]

When he arrived in the United States, Paz first spent some time in Los Angeles, where he had previously lived as a young boy.[2] As a child, according to his later claim in *Itinerary*,[3] he had felt a complete outsider in the Anglo-Saxon world. Now what immediately struck him was the way that the large immigrant Mexican

One of the first photographs of Paz as a Mexican diplomat.

community on the West coast had plainly left its imprint, and yet was so obviously not part of US culture. Paz identified with their predicament as finding themselves immersed in the modern world, and yet somehow not being part of it. Reflecting on this many years afterwards to his friend and colleague Enrique Krauze, he said: 'I recognised myself in them. I said to myself: 'I am them, and what has happened to my country in the modern world? Because what is happening to them is happening to all of us.'[4] Six years after his experiences in the Yucatán and Republican Spain, the poet no longer seems directly concerned with the political dimensions of his countrymen's predicament. There is no mention of their struggle to gain legal acceptance, or of the appalling conditions in which many of them had to work. Now it is the cultural, even mythical, dimensions of their presence in such an alien world that attracts his interest, and becomes the starting point for his most famous book, *El laberinto de la soledad* ('The Labyrinth of Solitude'), published at the end of the decade.[5]

After Los Angeles, Paz moved on to San Francisco and the University of California at Berkeley. In the following months he had the time to read poetry in English to his heart's desire. He caught up with all the poets who had come to be regarded as central in the first half of the twentieth century: W. B. Yeats, Ezra Pound, Wallace Stevens, e e cummings, William Carlos Williams and, of course, Eliot, of whom he later wrote: 'Modern man is a character from Eliot. Everything is alien for him and he recognizes himself in nothing. It's an expiation. Man is not a tree, nor a plant, nor a bird. He is alone in the middle of creation.'[6]

His stay on the West coast lasted more than a year. Towards the end of 1944, as his Guggenheim grant ran out, he was given a minor post in the Mexican diplomatic service as an assistant to the delegation from Mexico that was attending the inaugural sessions of the United Nations in San Francisco. By now, however, Paz was anxious to explore further, and wanted to move to the East coast and New York. In the summer of 1945, just as the war was ending, he taught Hispanic literature at Middlebury College in Vermont. There he made friends with the exiled Spanish poet Jorge Guillén, and took advantage of being close by to go and interview the elderly poet Robert Frost for the Argentine literary review *Sur*. After his teaching stint Paz spent a miserable winter in New York, enlivened mostly by visits to museums and art galleries, where he first started to develop his views on contemporary art. He did more work in the cinema, dubbing films into Spanish for Metro-Goldwyn-Meyer (thanks to an anarchist Spanish priest, with the daunting name of Padre Lobo, living in exile in New York). He apparently even tried to enlist for the US merchant marine, to travel but also perhaps to escape back to Europe again.

Octavio Paz in New York's Central Park, *c.* 1945.

However, 1945 ended with a crucial turning point in terms of employment. This came about, ironically enough, thanks to a close friend of his father's, Francisco Castillo Nájera, recently appointed Mexican Foreign Minister, who offered Paz the position of third secretary in the New York consulate. At the same time, Paz was offered the job of teaching Spanish once again. Apparently regarding a diplomatic career as a more secure proposition, Paz joined the Mexican foreign ministry. He was to remain part of it for the next 23 years: the young revolutionary, the man who had watched with dismay as the hopes of the Mexican revolution became stifled in the bureaucratic officialdom of the 1940s, represented this government loyally for more than two decades. As his close friend and assiduous biographer Guillermo Sheridan has pointed out: 'Little by little, he became yet another member of the new Mexican middle class, which was able to take advantage of the State's new needs in diplomacy, foreign trade, and public administration.'[7] In later life Paz was to explain that he saw no contradiction between his fierce defence of the writer's position as a rebel and his official position as representative of Mexico, because he was broadly in sympathy with his government's foreign policies. What the PRI government did within Mexico was a different matter, however, and this eventually led to him to quit the diplomatic service in protest in 1968.

The poems written during his time in the United States continue to reflect Paz's political and moral uncertainty. They form part of the collection *Puerta Condenada*, itself published as part of *Libertad bajo palabra* in 1949,[8] and reworked on several occasions by the poet. Poems such as 'Conscriptos' or 'Seven P.M.' show a new interest in narrative and everyday drama, while at the same time describing the solitude and lack of genuine values found in the modern city. This is Prufrock territory, inhabited by the timid, convention-bound creatures eking out their existence in the indifferent modern city, as described by T. S. Eliot and, before him, Jules Laforgue and Baudelaire. At the same time, in 'Conscriptos', for example, Paz incorporates snatches of the conversation heard around him: the raw material of life which poetry somehow has to accommodate and transcend. Elsewhere, Paz returns to the traditional sonnet form to express the spiritual emptiness of modern life, as reflected in the soulless streets of a city at dusk: 'Crepúsculo de la ciudad':

A la orilla, de mi ya desprendido
toco la destrucción que en mi se atreve
palpo ceniza y nada, lo que llueve
el cielo en su caer oscurecido

On the strand, already apart from me
I touch the destruction at work within
I feel ashes and nothingness, raining
from the darkened falling sky

However, it is in longer poems in the section 'Calamidades y Milagros' of *Libertad bajo palabra* that Paz's raw despair of the mid-1940s is most powerfully expressed. 'Soliloquio de medianoche' ('Midnight Soliloquy'), written in Berkeley in 1944, ranges over his personal beliefs, and how they have been emptied of meaning. Even the magic and purity of childhood with its infinite possibilities now seems to Paz to have come to nothing, while he finds it impossible to join in the activities that give life meaning for others – action and danger, or the defence of freedom 'on the distant battle-fronts'. The poem ends with him convinced only that everything is a sterile dream, from which there is no escape.

All these works are very different from the social protest and love poems of the 1930s; they speak of loneliness, despair and a lack of belief that poetry can change anything. Paz himself realized that he was trying to achieve something different at this stage of his writing, a vein which dried up when he was posted to the embassy in Paris at the end of 1945. Recalling his time in the United States, he wrote to the Catalan poet Pere Gimferrer in 1982: 'those poems had no continuation. There was a poet in me who did not manage to fully express himself.'[9]

The two years he spent in the United States marked Paz deeply. He never shared the anti-us feelings that were one of the essential attributes of 'progressive' Mexican intellectuals. Instead, he was greatly impressed by the way that United States society had embraced modernity, and was increasingly struck by the gap between the society built there and that of Mexico. The physical and psychological distance from his own country helped him to put that world into perspective, and to begin to reflect not only on what it meant to be Mexican, but on Mexico's place in the world and in history. These reflections were to lead to *El laberinto de la soledad*, published in 1950. Before then however, he was faced with a very different reality, when he returned to a Europe where, as he had rightly predicted, the war in Spain had been merely a prelude to a far more bitter and desperate fight against Fascism.

The Paris that Paz returned to in November 1945 was very different from the city he had so much enjoyed almost a decade earlier. In the intervening years France had seen military defeat by Hitler's Germany, followed by bitterly divisive years of occupation, collaboration and resistance. There were many shortages, and real hunger: the war damage throughout the country was intense, while the general mood was a complicated mixture of pride, hope, shame and despair. The Third Republic had collapsed, leaving a political vacuum. There was a struggle for power between the two main components of the Resistance: the fighters who were loyal to the French Communist party, and those who followed General Charles de Gaulle and his 'Free French' army. The possibility of civil violence dissipated when the general took firm political control in the immediate post-war period, while Moscow advised the French Communist Party to surrender its weapons. To Paz this situation was reminiscent not only of the Mexico of the early 1930s, with all the youthful debates he had taken part in as to how to broaden the revolution and make it truly socialist, but also of his experiences in Spain in 1937. During the immediate aftermath of the war writers and intellectuals were crucial to attempts to make sense of the past and to imagine a better future. In his *Collected Works*, Paz recalled this intellectual ferment, where he soon felt at home:

> I followed the philosophical and political debates closely. There was a tremendous atmosphere: a passion for ideas, for intellectual rigour . . . it was not long before I made friends who shared my intellectual and aesthetic concerns. I could breathe freely in

that cosmopolitan atmosphere: I was not from there, and yet I felt it was my intellectual home.[10]

But the literary and intellectual debates had also moved on from the days of his earlier visit. Already riven by internal disputes, the Surrealist movement of poets and painters was further split by the Second World War. Some members or former supporters stayed and joined the Resistance; others died trying to escape the Nazis, while André Breton and many of the painters spent the war years outside France. Like Paz, Breton returned to France soon after the conflict was over, but by this time a new literary movement had replaced Surrealism for the younger generation: this was Existentialism. In a similar way to the earlier movement, within a few years Existentialism came to mean almost anything to anyone, but in the immediate post-war years it was a response to the difficult questions thrown up by France's experience between 1939 and 1945: questions of freedom, the morality of direct action, the struggle between good and evil and the contingency of human life. The leaders of this movement, Jean-Paul Sartre, Simone de Beauvoir and Albert Camus, were novelists, short-story writers and also playwrights, rather than poets as the Surrealists were. It seemed that the literary mood in France had swung against poetry, possibly as part of a general mistrust of rhetoric of any kind.

In many respects, the debates and arguments between the two leading lights of existentialism, Sartre and Camus, took Paz back to what he had heard in Republican Spain. Sartre insisted that individual freedom only made sense when it became part of a larger political struggle, and that Marxism offered the best chance of that struggle bringing about revolutionary change to a society that had been proven politically and morally bankrupt. Albert Camus was less openly political, and founded his hopes for the future on individual revolt, which would lead to solidarity and genuine political change based on moral values. As well as being a writer of fiction,

Octavio Paz in Surrealist mode, Paris, 1949.

Sartre sought to base his existentialism on laboriously argued philosophical tracts that went back to nineteenth-century German rationalist philosophers in an effort to define human identity in an uncaring world dominated by time. Camus, on the other hand, preferred literary essays that drew on his wide but unsystematic reading from the past. He had published *Le mythe de Sisyphe* ('The Myth of Sisyphus') in 1942, and was working on *L'Homme revolté*, another long essay that struck many chords with the Mexican poet. Like Paz, Camus was closely interested in Spain, and the possibility of ousting Franco and restoring the Republic there: the two men in fact met in 1946 at an act of homage to the Spanish poet Antonio Machado, who had died in miserable exile in the south of France in

1939. Born in French Algeria, Camus also had a similarly complex relationship with France and its culture as Paz did with Mexico. Above all, it was Camus' moral honesty that the Mexican writer admired, based as it was on a recognition of the 'absurdity' of human existence, and a refusal to turn to religion, politics or even art for an easy solution.

For Paz, the decisive moment in the debate between these two lines of thought came in 1949. David Rousset was a French prisoner in the Nazi camps who in 1946 had described his experiences in a devastating book *L'univers concentrationnaire* ('The Concentration Camp World'). In 1949 he followed this up with an equally damning denunciation of the Soviet labour camp system, and started an international protest campaign against them. This was at the height of the Cold War, and his anti-Soviet attitude aroused a huge furore in radical French circles: Sartre and Aragon claimed Rousset must be an 'imperialist spy'. Other writers, including Paz, were forced to take sides. As ever, Paz reacted against the idea that that it was the responsibility of 'progressive' intellectuals to back the Soviet Union because 'objectively' it was less repressive than the capitalist system: as in Spain, he denounced those whose political loyalties obscured the truth. This again alienated him from poets such as Neruda and other more orthodox Marxist writers. When Paz translated parts of Rousset's articles, he found he could not publish them in Mexico, and in the end turned to the influential Argentine magazine *Sur*, which published them in 1951. Paz's sombre conclusion to Rousset's revelations was that 'The problem of the Soviet camps raises the question of the real historical meaning of the Russian state and its inability to resolve the social contradictions of capitalism in favour of the productive classes.'[11]

Although Paz admired Camus, Roger Caillois and other French writers of the time, it was the Surrealist 'pope' André Breton to whom the Mexican writer felt closest in spirit. In the late 1930s Paz had been wary of Breton's alliance with Leon Trotsky in Mexico, but he now came to admire the French poet's instinctive rejection of authority, his espousal of individual freedom based on the power of desire and his innate distrust of political orthodoxies. Poetically, Paz shared Breton's belief in the power of images to communicate a different and essential level of reality, and also that poetry was not a question of form, but of a moral stance towards life. Introduced to him in Paris by Benjamin Péret, who had spent some of the war years in Mexico and translated some of Paz's poems, the two men soon became close friends. So great was the influence of the French writer on Paz, not only in these Paris years but through the rest of his writing career, that when Breton died he wrote: 'I often write as though I were engaging in a silent dialogue with Breton; countering him, replying to him, coinciding with him, diverging from him, writing a homage to him – all this together.'[12]

At the same time, Paz was able to renew contacts with the sizeable Latin American literary community living in post-war Paris, in particular the Cuban novelist Alejo Carpentier, the Argentine writer Adolfo Bioy Casares and Blanca Varela, the young Peruvian poet, together with her painter husband Fernando de Syszlo. He continued his friendship with the exiled Spanish film-maker Luis Buñuel, who had settled in Mexico in 1946 and become a Mexican citizen in 1949. In 1951 Paz accompanied Buñuel to the Cannes film festival to help promote his film *Los Olvidados* ('The Forgotten Ones'). Although this was to become one of Buñuel's most famous and admired films, at the time its harsh portrayal of those left on the margins of society in post-revolutionary Mexico led to its being disowned by the Mexican government. Despite his official position, Paz distributed his defence of Buñuel ('Buñuel el poeta') outside the cinema showing the film, and although he was not sanctioned, this and his outspoken support for the Spanish Republic (at a commemorative act in July 1951) probably led to the decision by Mexican Foreign ministry officials that it was time he moved on from Paris.

The stimulus Paz received from the intellectual life in Paris, the support from Breton and the Surrealist group, as well as his Latin American literary friends and champions such as Alfonso Reyes back in Mexico, all encouraged Paz to go on writing despite his doubts as to its worth. In fact, the end of this decade saw him bring out three books that are not only centrally important to his work as a whole, but to Mexican and Hispanic literature in the second half of the twentieth century. These books were *Libertad bajo palabra* ('Freedom On Parole'), a book of poems published in Mexico in 1949,[13] the essay *El laberinto de la soledad*, which came out in 1950,[14] and the prose collection *¿Aguila o sol?* ('Eagle or Sun?'), which first appeared in 1951.[15]

The first published version of *Libertad bajo palabra* comprised 74 poems. As with much of his work, Paz revisited the collection quite often, changing texts, leaving some poems out and bringing others in. The 1960 edition describes the common theme of all the poems as 'affinities of theme, colour, rhythm, intonation or atmosphere.' The overall shape of the 1949 book (originally to have been called *Todavía* ('Still', or 'Yet', a defiant assertion that the author is still writing despite all that he has lived through since his last major publication in 1942) has been described by Enrico Mario Santí as a sonata, with three movements: a central *allegro* section flanked by two darker sections.[16] As the prose poem which gives the collection its title indicates, Paz here is concerned with how the art of poetry (*la palabra*) can lead to freedom: it is an essential means to achieving it and yet, as the play on words suggests, the freedom won must always be provisional. By now Paz the poet no longer believes that revolution, Marxist or otherwise, can bring about individual or collective freedom. The starting point, as Breton had shown him, must come through the freeing of the individual conscience and the expression of this transformation in art. By example, the poet can perhaps offer others a glimpse of liberation. To do this, the poet must work in the 'zone where interior and exterior coincide: the zone of language' as Paz wrote in *Los hijos del limo*. Language, and the possibilities for freedom that it offers, is 'something given and something we create. Something that creates us . . .'.[17]

This sensibility is particularly evident in the long poem 'Himno entre ruinas' ('Hymn in the Midst of Ruins') written in Naples in 1948. Here Paz's interest in colloquial speech and the creation of simultaneous narratives leads him to juxtapose four different voices in what he called 'a unique space: the central voice of the poem'.[18] Despite the ruins all around him, and the poet's sense of isolation and solitude, the value of language and poetry can be triumphantly asserted in the last lines of the poem: 'Hombre, árbol de imágenes,/ palabras que son flores que son frutos que son actos' ('Man, tree of images/ words that are flowers that are fruits that are deeds').

Another key poem from 1948 is 'El Prisionero' ('The Prisoner'), dedicated to the Marquis de Sade. The eighteenth-century French philosopher was considered an essential precursor by Breton and the other Surrealists because of his violent defence of sexual and political freedoms. A visit to his castle at Lacoste near Avignon was one of their favourite pilgrimages, and Paz appears to have been there too, as the poem is recorded as being written in Avignon, and contains a description of the castle. Yet Paz's view of Sade is more nuanced than Breton's. After assessing Sade's continuing importance in the twentieth century, Paz concludes that Sade's eroticism has led him to become trapped in a hall of mirrors : 'Prisionero en tu castillo de cristal de roca' ('A prisoner in your rock-crystal castle'), a prison from which he cannot escape because it is an entirely selfish quest from which any other person is excluded. For Paz, it is the ability of erotic love to transcend individual contingency that is all-important: as he puts it in this poem: 'Sólo en mi semejante me trasciendo/ solo su sangre da fe de otra existencia' ('Only in my fellow can I transcend myself/ only their blood testifies to another existence'). At the same time, however, in these long flowing lines Paz recognizes that this Sadean obsession with self is also part of his own make-up, and although the poem concludes with an exhortation to have the courage to recognize that 'la libertad es la elección de la necesidad' ('freedom is the choice of necessity') the very final line returns us to Sade's face constantly dissolving and reforming in his 'diamond castle'.

At the same time as Paz was exploring the French literary and philosophical traditions, the distance from his home country also raised questions for him about Mexican identity and Mexico's place in the world. Although this appears in many poems, it is above all in the series of linked essays of *El laberinto de la soledad* that the investigation is most complete The book had several origins. While still living in Mexico in the early 1940s, Paz had written a weekly column in the newspaper *Novedades*. Although many of the articles dealt with political and cultural topics of the moment, some also reflected on aspects of Mexican history and identity. In addition, as we have seen, Paz was also jolted into a recognition of Mexican-ness by what he saw of his compatriots on the West coast of the United States. As he was to write in *El laberinto*, the Mexican migrant *pachucos* (what today would be called the 'chicanos') with their zoot suits and extravagant hairstyles, were immediately recognizable and stood out from their sober Anglo-Saxon surroundings:

Their Mexican-ness – a taste for decoration, laxness and splendour, negligence, passion and reserve – floats in the air. I say it floats because it does not get mixed or confused with the other world, the North American world, made of precision and efficiency. It floats, but it does not contradict; it hovers, pushed on the wind, sometimes torn apart like a cloud, at others erect like a climbing rocket. It crawls, withdraws in on itself, expands, contracts, sleeps or dreams, a beauty in tatters. It floats: it is never quite born, or ever quite vanishes.[19]

This extract shows how far Paz's essay on solitude is that of a poet rather than a historian. His observations on the Mexican character are a mixture of poetic insight, vivid images and sweeping generalizations. Unlike Sartre or Camus he is not offering a general treatise on human existence; instead, he concentrates on the drama of what it means to be Mexican in the modern world. Another source of *El laberinto*, as Paz told the Spanish writer Julián Ríos in 1972, was the 'Mexican' novel he had tried to write in the mid-1940s. The starting point for this seems to have been D. H. Lawrence's novel set in Mexico, *The Plumed Serpent,* where the protagonists struggle to understand the to them utterly alien worlds of the indigenous Mexicans and the *mestizo* culture. Paz attempted to write a novel that would redefine these characteristics from a more authentically Mexican point of view, but as he explained to Ríos, his efforts never saw the light of day: 'It was a pastiche of Lawrence, so I decided to destroy it . . . I destroyed it because the characters talked like *El laberinto*; I realized that the only interesting thing was what the characters were saying.'[20]

It was not until 1948–9 that Paz sat down to actually write the book, and there is no doubt that the French 'moralist' tradition of essays, from Montaigne (whom Paz read and recommended during these years) to Albert Camus, was another strand of influence. So too were books on myth such as Robert Caillois' *Le mythe et l'homme,* which Paz is known to have read and admired. The most intense period of work on the book came in the summer of 1949, as Paz recalled in an introduction published in his *Collected Works*:

> The city was deserted and my work in the Mexican embassy, where I held a modest post, had diminished. The distance helped: I was living in a world far from Mexico and was protected from its phantoms. I had my Friday afternoons and the whole of Saturdays and Sundays free. And the nights. I wrote quickly and fluently, anxious to finish, as though a revelation was awaiting me on the last page of the book. I was running a race against myself. Who are what was I going to find at the finishing line? I knew the question, but not the answer. Writing

became a contradictory ceremony, a mixture of enthusiasm and rage, sympathy and anguish. As I wrote, I was taking revenge on Mexico; then an instant later my writing would turn against me, and Mexico was taking its revenge on me. An inextricable knot, made up of passion and lucidity. *Love and hate.*[21]

El laberinto is Paz's answer to two questions: what it means to be Mexican in the twentieth century, after the revolution which brought Mexico into world history, and what does Mexico mean in the world? The solitude of the title refers to both Mexico's isolation from the rest of the world for much of its history, and also the existential solitude that by the late 1940s Paz considered to be an essential part of the human condition. The first four chapters of the book look at different aspects of Mexican identity. These all illustrate how the Mexican 'temperament' shows its solitude, from the *pachucos* of Los Angeles to Mexican male attitudes towards women, from La Malinche (the legendary interpreter for the Spanish conquistador Hernán Cortes, here seen as the ambivalent mother of the Mexican nation) onwards. The second half of the book is what Paz termed a 'morally critical review' of Mexico's history: the first two chapters deal with the conquest by the Spaniards and Mexico's independence struggle, followed by the years of revolution, which Paz sees as Mexico finally coming to terms with its complex heritage; the second two chapters place Mexico in the modern world and attempt to define twentieth-century, post-revolutionary Mexicans in a rapidly shifting panorama. As usual with Paz, he tinkered with the text, and in 1959 a second, revised, edition appeared. This second edition also includes an important addition: *La dialéctica de la soledad* ('The Dialectics of Solitude'), in which Paz responds to critics of his book by adding an explanation of his approach and main concerns. Here Paz suggests a way out of solitude (a possibility that was available to him in the late 1950s, but not earlier) through the mutual surrender of the loving couple. By this willing abandonment of individuality,

A work by Rufino Tamayo, one of the first artists about whom Paz wrote extensively.

Paz suggests we can glimpse freedom, and the kind of redemption that could save us from the labyrinth.

When the first edition of *El laberinto* appeared in Mexico, it did not become an immediate success. Enrico Mario Santí has found only five reviews of it, none of them substantial.[22] But the book soon stirred up a polemic, and its second edition in particular drew fierce criticism. Paz was attacked from the nationalist side: he was almost a foreigner, some of his critics claimed, and so could not possibly understand the Mexican character. (Paradoxically, in his book Paz had hit on this method of disqualifying one's adversary by the process of '*ningunear*'– destroying their legitimacy – as precisely one of the most salient features of the Mexican character). He was also accused of giving a very negative view of Mexicans, for revealing 'the Mexican's sense of shame for existing'. Others rounded on him for allegedly not acknowledging his debt to predecessors such as Samuel Ramos, who had probed the Mexican psyche in the early 1930s.

In spite of these criticisms *El laberinto* has become the book Paz that is best known for, in Mexico and internationally. Over the past fifty years, it has become a touchstone for debates about Mexican identity in a changing world, as well as providing literary inspiration for novelists such as Juan Rulfo and Carlos Fuentes. It is perhaps also no coincidence that the other most famous Latin American book of the last half century, the Colombian writer Gabriel García Márquez's *Cien años de soledad* (*One Hundred Years of Solitude*) should also be concerned with the way that history appears to have condemned Latin America to isolation and exclusion. *El laberinto* has become a set text in Mexican secondary schools, and is the work that has been most translated. Paz has stressed how personal the book was for him. In a 1990 TV interview, for example, he said: 'Reflecting on the strangeness of being Mexican, I discovered an old truth: every man hides a stranger,

The cover of a paperback edition of Paz's *El laberinto de la soledad*.

every man is inhabited by a ghost. I wanted to get inside myself and dig up that stranger, to talk with him. My book is not a sociological or psychological treatise. What is it then? A confession, or rather a declaration . . .'. [23] Reading this, it is hard not to see *El laberinto* as also being a response to his father and grandfather. They may have made history by their actions, but Paz now takes on history in his writing, and in so doing justifies his own existence alongside theirs.

Paz's third major publication while he was still living in Paris was the collection of prose poems *¿Aguila o sol?* ('Eagle or Sun?' – the Mexican equivalent of heads or tails on a coin). In exchanging his earlier lyrical poetry for these prose poems, Paz adopted the Surrealist conviction that true poetry is not a question of form, but of a moral attitude towards life, to be expressed in whatever means seems best suited to the writer's experience. The tradition of the prose poem in French literature goes back to Baudelaire and Rimbaud, and was much cultivated by writers close to Surrealism such as Henri Michaux or René Char, but the Paz poems retain a narrative structure and although they delve into the subconscious and are in no way the kind of automatic writing typical of more impenetrable Surrealist texts. The three sections of *¿Aguila o sol?* consider first of all the struggle of the poet to create something new from language, described as a fight against the most gruesome monsters that seek to distort or maim his ability to be able to give new meaning to words so often cheapened by daily commerce. Once the possibility of poetic discovery has been won, the second part of the collection, 'Arenas movedizas' ('Quicksands') turns to the outside world, and the figure of the poet in relation to others. The most striking poem here is the opening one, 'El ramo azul' ('The Blue Bouquet'). Here Paz's nightmare of being hunted for his blue (foreigner's) eyes by a Mexican Indian peasant reveals all his anxieties about his identity, doubts made all the sharper by his immersion in the sophisticated cosmopolitan city world of Paris.

The third section of prose poems, which shares a title with the collection as a whole, further explores the poet's relation to the other: this time the stranger is his childhood self, but also the buried pre-Columbian past of Mexico. Included here is the poem 'Mariposa de obsidiana' ('Obsidian Butterfly'), the lament of the pre-Columbian goddess Itzpapálotl for all she has lost with the Conquest, a poem first published in French and included in André Breton's anthology of Surrealist poetry of the first half of the twentieth century. Despite the violence and despair evident from many poems in this collection, it ends on a more positive note with 'Hacia el poema' ('Towards the Poem'). This again posits the idea that the creation of poetry is essential for any possibility of dialogue between solitary individuals, and concludes with a challenge to history: 'When History sleeps, it talks in its dreams; in the mind of the sleeping people the poem is a constellation of blood. When History awakens, the image becomes deed, and the poem occurs: poetry enters into action.'

This preoccupation with defining the poet's position in relation to history is also evident in a 1950 anthology of Mexican poetry which Paz was commissioned to produce for the recently established UNESCO.[24] Paz included 35 poets writing in Spanish, starting in 1521 and including only one contemporary: his master and protector, Alfonso Reyes, the poet from an earlier generation who had supported and encouraged Paz throughout his career. In his succinct introduction, Paz traces a linear progress of Mexican poetry, demonstrating the enthusiasms that were to last him a lifetime, especially for the work of Juan José Tablada and the eighteenth-century Mexican nun Sor Juana. Although the remit of the anthology meant he had to exclude members of his own generation, Paz's introduction ends with a consideration of what he saw as the important task facing poets of his generation: the relation between poetry and history. Here his conclusion is that 'every poem is an attempt to reconcile history and poetry for the benefit of poetry . . .

There can be no poetry without history, but poetry has no other mission than to transmute history. And therefore the only true revolutionary poetry is apocalyptic poetry.' The anthology was also published in English, which led Paz to meet the translator, none other than the Irish writer Samuel Beckett, another resident of post-war Paris. This makes the anthology unique as having been produced by two men later to become Nobel Literature prize-winners, although this appears to have been their only literary collaboration.

Parallel to the prose poems, Paz was also writing verse. The poems from the late 1940s and early 1950s were later collected into *La estación violenta* ('The Violent Season'), published in Mexico in 1958.[25] The collection begins with the previously mentioned 'Himno entre ruinas', written in Naples in 1948, and ends with one of his masterpieces from the mid-1950s, 'Piedra de sol' ('Sunstone'). These poems, which will be looked at in more detail in the next chapter, see Paz gradually emerging from what he described as the dark 'tunnel' of the years in Paris, as his personal circumstances changed and he once more began to explore another, even more distant, civilization. At first though, his view of this upheaval was not at all positive. As he wrote at the end of 1951 to Alfonso Reyes back in Mexico:

Although I try to console myself thinking of the fabulous but atrocious reality of India, I cannot get over my pain. Leaving Paris is not easy. Besides which, I think it's a mistake to move me now. They're moving me just when I was starting to be useful, when the French were beginning to realize I exist.[26]

Paz was posted to New Delhi, where Mexico was setting up an embassy in the recently independent India. He left his wife, Elena Garro, and daughter in Paris, and set off by boat for the new continent. This sense of loss made it hard for him to come to terms with

Paz with Elena Garro and friends, Japan, 1952.

a country that later was to become so important for him. He found the official work difficult, and greatly missed the intellectual stimulus of Paris, complaining in one letter that he is 'enclosed in this diplomatic island . . . where there aren't many pretty women, or intelligent people among my new colleagues'.[27] He was soon trying to secure a diplomatic return to Mexico, although he was also beginning to turn his stay in India to poetic advantage, as in the poem 'Mutra'. Here, as often in his long poems, Paz starts with a vivid description of the heat and overwhelming throng of humanity in the holy city of Mutra; then moving on to his inner world, and what his poetic conscience has made of this new confrontation with the teeming world of appearances. What emerges is an implicit rejection of Eastern religious beatitude: as a poet from the European tradition, it is his duty to try to interpret the world for others, not to retire into one of his own. 'Man is only a man among men', he concludes.

Instead of an immediate return to Mexico, after six months in India Paz was dispatched to an even more remote posting, this time to Japan, where he spent several months. Once again, the adaptation seems to have been difficult: he wrote to Mexico complaining he did not have enough money or staff, and when Elena and his daughter arrived from Paris, they all had to live in one hotel room. Matters became even worse when his wife fell seriously ill, and the ill-guided attempts at a cure left her temporarily paralysed from the waist down. In this emergency the whole family was evacuated to Switzerland so that Elena could be treated, and by the end of 1953 Paz and his family were back in Mexico. The most important poem Paz wrote during his stay in Japan reflects the grimness of his mood at the time: '¿No hay salida?' ('Is there no way out?').

Even though this ending to nine years spent living outside Mexico was a bitter disappointment, Paz later looked back on the experience in a much more positive light. Those years, he said, were like 'nine months lived in the belly of time, a period of gestation. I was born again and the person who returned to Mexico in 1953 was another poet, another writer.'[28]

4

Reaching Out, 1953–69

Nearing his fortieth birthday, Octavio Paz returned to Mexico City. His mother was still living in Mixcoac, but that town had now been incorporated into the sprawling metropolis, whose population had grown from less than one million in his childhood to over five million by the start of the 1950s. The revolutionary hopes of Paz's youth had also disappeared, swallowed up by the all-encompassing rule of the PRI, which continued successfully to bestow patronage and benefits in return for political loyalty. Mexico had emerged from the Second World War in a favourable economic position, with growing exports and a burgeoning national industry. As president from 1946 to 1952, Miguel Alemán used these favourable conditions to consolidate what was virtually a one-party system.[1] His PRI government embarked upon massive new infrastructure projects to convey this new sense of national pride, as well as promising every Mexican (in his words): 'a Cadillac, a cigar, and a ticket to the bullfight'. The new projects included the first expressways through the capital, while a reorganization of the historic centre meant that the thousands of students attending the National Autonomous University were moved out of the heart of the city, where Paz himself had studied, to a specially built campus in the south. Although one of the aims of this move may well have been to remove a potential source of political protest, the ever-growing numbers of students soon converted their new home into a hotbed of revolutionary debate, especially after the Cuban revolution in 1959, and it was the tragic outcome to one of their most determined political campaigns that was to lead to Paz's resignation from the Mexican Foreign Service in 1968.

In 1953, however, he was content to continue his diplomatic career back in Mexico. After his return from India, this took a new turn, when he was named as Head of International Organizations, which involved him in developing Mexico's representation in bodies such as the United Nations and UNESCO, of which he already had considerable experience. However, Paz's return was not universally celebrated in Mexican literary circles. He was accused by the ever-present nationalists (whether from the PRI or groups further to the left) of selling out to 'foreign' influences because of his enthusiasm for Surrealism, which he outlined in an important lecture in Mexico City in 1954.[2] Others accused him of writing about Mexico in a denigrating way (particularly in the essays of *El laberinto*) because he was a cultural snob who preferred to live abroad, and had therefore also disqualified himself from writing about it. Others were simply jealous of his growing international recognition as a poet. Paz himself declared to the translator Alfred Macadam in 1990:

> My return was not a reconciliation. On the contrary, I was only accepted by a few youngsters. I had broken free of the dominant aesthetic, moral and political ideas, and it was not long before I came under attack from a lot of people, who were only too sure of their dogmas and prejudices. That was the start of a disagreement that has never ended.[3]

The disagreement immediately showed itself in the reception of *Semillas para un himno* ('Seeds for a Hymn'),[4] the first collection Paz published after returning to Mexico. Many local critics accused his new poetry of being hermetic, and of being 'contaminated' by European Surrealism. They compared the violent, complex imagery unfavourably with his earlier, more socially explicit, work.

Avenida Reforma, Mexico City, 1950s.

Not everyone was hostile, however, and a significant number of young poets reacted favourably to Paz's attempts to forge a new language – the 'seeds' for a new vision of the poet's possibilities. They were receptive to the idea that poetic language based on the power of metaphor could suggest that reality might be meaningfully not simply transcended but changed in favour of a freer, more hopeful world.[5]

Among the new friends that Paz gathered around him in Mexico City was the novelist Carlos Fuentes.[6] Born in Panama of a diplomat father, Fuentes was, like Paz himself, someone who regarded narrow Mexican nationalism as abhorrent. Paz was involved in helping

Fuentes found an important new review, the *Revista mexicana de literatura*, in which the poet published several of his new poems. Others who began to form a group of like-minded writers around Paz were Ramón Xirau, Juan Rulfo and especially Elena Poniatowska. She first interviewed him in January 1954 and wrote an enthusiastic biographical sketch on his death in 1998.[7] Her vivid description of what it was like to debate a topic with the poet is worth recalling: 'anyone who takes you on always comes out bruised, dishevelled, ends up like a dishcloth, even though you are not really that bothered about always coming out on top . . . The main thing for you is to contradict, to exchange certainties, because you know that argument is always fruitful.'[8] Equally interesting for the political rhetoric it displays is Paz's combative response to Poniatowska's final question in that first interview, concerning the relationship between writer and public in Mexico:

> The writer, as such, has no obligation . . . to try to directly improve the situation of the country. We all have social obligations, but the writer has a further obligation; to tell the truth (as he sees it) even if that seems scandalous or disagreeable. We need to assert our right to be disagreeable. For example, to dare to shake the Mexican bourgeoisie up a little. All the so-comfortably seated bourgeoisie: the society ladies enthroned in their respectability and virtue; the politicians in their power; the bankers and their money; the leaders in their lies. In fact, they are all seated on the poverty of the people.[9]

This anger at the 'beastly bourgeosie' is also obvious in the most powerful of the poems Paz wrote in the early years of his return to Mexico, 'El cántaro roto' ('The Broken Jar'). This was first published in Fuentes' *Revista mexicana de literatura* and collected in *La estación violenta* ('The Violent Season') published in 1958.[10] *El cántaro roto* is a long work partly inspired by a trip Paz made in 1954 through the dry deserts of northern Mexico. Coming into contact with the desperate rural poverty of his home country after so many years away aroused Paz's indignation at how little progress had been made since the revolution. His poem looks at the way that any possibility of freshness (life-giving water) has been destroyed yet again by greed and ignorance. The first section is an exploration of the poet's inner world and all its riches but, as so often in Paz, he quickly concludes that it is not enough for the poet to be satisfied with this: it is necessary for him to also look outwards and not remain in the inner realm. That outer world can seem exciting and harmonious but, once again, Paz portrays this romantic vision of nature as a trap for the poet and, by extension, any aware human being. A less enchanted approach to the world will inevitably show it to be dry as dust:

> *No cantaba el grillo*
> *Había un vago olor a cal y semillas quemadas*
> *Las calles del poblado eran arroyos secos*
> *Y el aire se habría roto en mil pedazos si alguien hubiese gritado:*
> *¿quien vive?*

> The cricket did not sing
> There was a vague smell of burnt lime and seeds
> The streets of the village were dried up rivers
> And the air would have smashed into a thousand pieces had any
> one shouted: Who's alive here?[11]

The lack of life and hope in the outside world threatens to reduce the poet to a state of paralysing despair, reducing him to silence. Once again, it is anger which helps him overcome this paralysis, and in particular the disgust that the only creature able to rule in this dusty landscape is the 'sapo' – the toad that represents the ugly aspects of power. The toad has been around since before the

Spaniards, and was personified by the 'Lord of Cempoala', the local chieftain who betrayed the Aztecs to Hernán Cortés. In the final 22 lines of the poem the sense of despair is triumphantly dispelled in a long list of exhortations to himself and his readers, beginning with the formula 'Hay que' 'one must': 'dream with open eyes, dream with one's hands, dream out loud' to restore the possibilities of life and fertility in this barren landscape. Whereas in the 1930s the shock of underdevelopment in the Yucatán had led the young poet to a condemnation of capitalism and all its works, now the emphasis is on personal responsibility, and the responsibility of poetry, to offer a life-giving alternative.

Part of this effort to take poetry out into the world saw Paz experimenting with other genres. While in Japan, he had been fascinated by the modern No plays put on by Yukio Mishima. Back in Mexico, and encouraged by Jaime García Terres, head of the Autonomous University's Cultural Diffusion programme, he and his friends, including the painter Juan Soriano and the Surrealist painter Leonora Carrington, put on what they described as 'poesía en voz alta' ('poetry out loud'), a theatrical adventure whose aim Paz declared as: 'to bring back the air of mystery to the stage: a ritual game and a spectacle that included the audience'.[12] The theatre festival included eight pieces, with works by Jean Genet, Ionesco and Paz's wife Elena Garro. Paz himself wrote *La hija de Rappaccini,* a one-act poetic drama based on a story by Nathaniel Hawthorne. First put on at the Teatro del Caballito in Mexico City in 1956, when it was directed by Héctor Mendoza, the work was later made into an opera and performed in 1989, this time directed by Daniel Gatán. In Paz's play a student falls in love with a young girl (Rappaccini's daughter) when he sees her in a garden outside his window. Rappaccini is a scientist who uses the poison from flowers for his dubious experiments. His daughter has been brought up for so long in this atmosphere that she only has to breathe on animals and flowers for them to die. Irresistibly attracted to the girl, the student ventures into the garden: she does not harm him but, as his visits to her multiply, he finds that he too can cause the death of living beings around him. When he accuses her of treachery, she points out no harm has come to him, but he insists she drink an antidote to the poisons and, when she does so, she dies. The play mystified many Mexican critics, and with its high-flown poetic language, references to the Tarot and a variety of myths, it shows that Paz might see literature as of vital importance to life, but this does not mean that (as in his youthful adventures in Spain) it should be directly accessible to 'the people'.[13]

In addition to these experiments, Paz was still reflecting on the nature of poetry itself. What were its specific characteristics, what made its message different from anything else, and what possibilities did it offer? In 1956, thanks to a grant from the Colegio de Mexico, he was able to spend time writing the extended essay that was published as *El arco y la lira* ('The Bow and the Lyre').[14] The title is taken from Heraclitus, and suggests that poetry can be static, producing its music as do the strings of the lyre, while at the same time having a dynamic function, the ability to shoot out into the world as the arrow does from the bowstring, to explore the otherness of the world outside the individual consciousness.

El arco y la lira is in three parts. The first looks at what Paz defines as the essence of poetry, and then considers the specific formal characteristics of poetry. The second part looks at 'poetic revelation', and is the heart of the book. As in his 1942 essay inspired by reflections on the work of the Spanish mystic San Juan de la Cruz, the central question of Paz's new essay is to identify what constitutes poetic revelation, and to suggest how this differs from religious experience. The chief difference, as Rafael Argullol suggests in his consideration of Paz's book, is their relationship to death. In Paz's view, the religious approach to death leads to a lessening of the importance of human 'being' in this world, because it needs an all-powerful entity beyond death to give life meaning.

Only the divine can be said to truly exist, and human life is lacking (or is 'sinful') because it does not live up to the plenitude of this divine. According to Paz:

> Religion redeems us from death, but in so doing makes life on earth a prolonged suffering and an expiation for original sin. By killing death, religion deprives life of life. Eternity pushes out the instant. Because life and death are inseparable. Death is part of life: we live dying. And every minute we die, we live. By robbing us of death, religion robs us of life.[15]

By contrast, Paz argues poetry offers mankind the chance of bringing the contradictions of life and death into harmony. The poet asserts life and assumes death as an integral part of it: so hope becomes an integral part of life and is no longer located outside it in a supreme being. In this sense, following Holderlin and the German Romantics, Paz asserts that 'it is as a poet that man inhabits the earth'.

The third section of *El arco y la lira* looks at how poetry can make an impact on the world beyond the individual consciousness. In his poetics Paz argues that poetry attempts to abolish 'the distance between the word and the thing . . .'. Modern poetry moves between two poles, the magical and the revolutionary. The magical pull consists in a desire to return to nature by dissolving the self-consciousness that separates us from it, to 'lose oneself forever in animal innocence, or to liberate oneself from history'. The revolutionary aspiration demands 'a conquest of the historical world and of nature'. Fundamentally, both these approaches are ways of bridging the gap and reconciling the 'alienated consciousness' to the world outside.[16]

At the same time as he was writing this long essay on poetry, Paz completed *Piedra de sol* ('Sunstone'), regarded by many as one of his finest works. The Catalan poet Pere Gimferrer (who was to become a close friend of the Mexican poet) sees it as important in the Hispanic world as Eliot's *The Waste Land* was for the English-language world: 'a substantial part of the new literary avant-garde in Latin America and Spain – and not just in the field of poetry, but also in the novel and the essay . . . is only properly understood thanks to its existence'.[17] For his part, the Argentine writer Julio Cortázar praised it as 'the most admirable love poem ever written in Latin America, the response in the realm of erotic love to mankind's thirst for total confrontation with his own transcendence',[18] while a Mexican poet from the next generation, José Emilio Pacecho, has written of how it galvanized the poetic research he and his companions were undertaking in Mexico as they started out as poets.[19] Pacheco also includes the end-note published by Paz in the first edition of the poem but omitted from all subsequent versions.[20] Here Paz explains that the poem has 584 lines because this was the period of the Mayan calendar based on the observation of Venus. He also notes that Venus appears in the sky at both evening and morning, and this basic ambiguity between the end of life and its beginning informs the poem in many ways. The huge, circular sunstone itself is not Mayan but Aztec, however: it was reportedly buried by the Spaniards when they conquered Mexico, and only discovered again in 1790 under the cathedral in Mexico's central square.[21] Paz above all takes from the sunstone calendar its combination of linear time and circularity, which is represented in the poem by the last six lines being the same as the first six: we move through the poem, but come back to the beginning and start again (hence also the quotation from Gérard de Nerval's *Les Chimères* at the start of the work: 'la treizième revient . . . c'est encore la première'.

Piedra de sol was by far Paz's most ambitious poem to date. It is an attempt to embody all the ideas about the possibilities of poetry which he wrote about in *El arco y la lira* in a single poem, attempting to convince the reader on an entirely different level to that of the essay. While it contains autobiographical details from Paz's life, it is also a consideration of different periods of history, and makes reference to many myths from classical Greece as well as France and Mexico. What is most noticeable about the poem's atmosphere is that Paz appears to be finally emerging from the doubts and despair so obvious during his years in Paris and the early days after going back to Mexico. Although it is dangerous to reduce the emotions of the poem to events in his private life, *Piedra de sol* does coincide with the appearance of a new great love. This was Bona Tibertelli de Pisis,[22] who, when Paz first met her in Switzerland in 1953, was married to the French writer André Pieyre de Mandiargues. On one level at least, the poem can be seen as an offering to this new love, as a way of trying to explain to a newcomer in his life just what he believes can redeem existence from the ordinary corrosive passage of time. The poem embodies the belief that truth can be discovered at the moment of the ecstasy of erotic love, and sees this moment as wiping out the whole of history as it renews innocence. Simultaneously though, thanks to the union with someone else, engagement with the world of time becomes not merely possible but a moral imperative for the poet. Through love he rediscovers his essential oneness with the world around him, while at the same time he regains his faith that language can triumphantly convey the uniqueness of this discovery. *Piedra de sol* convinces through its imagery, through the constant sinuous movement of the lines and thoughts, and through the almost incantatory effect of the spiralling progress of the verses. Nothing in the poem is stable: lines and thoughts and images rush along, like the river of time or the fluidity of identity which leads him to proclaim in his moment of triumph: 'adonde yo soy tu somos nosotros' ('where I am you are we').

Piedra de sol was included as the final poem in the 1958 collection *La estación violenta* ('The Violent Season'). Together with 'El cántaro roto' it forms a counterpoint to earlier works written during his travels in Europe, adding all that Paz had experienced since his return to Mexico. In 1960, these and many of his earlier works were collected in *Libertad bajo palabra* ('Freedom on Parole').[23] Commenting on this collection of his early work in 1979, Paz explained the paradox of the title in terms of man's essential freedom being conditioned by art and, in particular, poetry. On the one hand he rejects the idea that poetry is born spontaneously, or is the direct transcription of dreams, while on the other arguing that it cannot be the product of thought alone. He concludes that the meeting point of the work of art is the embodiment of this kind of 'conditional freedom': 'conditional because spontaneity is achieved not outside form but within it and through it'.[24] Paz's wish to gather and take stock of what he had achieved as a poet was the prelude not only to a fresh leap out of Mexico, but also to great changes in his personal life.

His involvement with Bona Tibertelli grew during a visit she and her husband made to Mexico in March 1958. Paz arranged trips for the couple, and exhibitions of Bona's art works. So strong was the attraction that Paz was determined to follow her back to Paris. A first opportunity arose in November of the same year, when he was invited as a diplomat to the tenth anniversary celebrations for UNESCO. Soon after this came divorce from Elena Garro, and a desperate wait to return to Paris on a more permanent basis, in order to be with Bona and to start afresh. The split from his wife was not easy, as she turned violently against him. We will see later her alleged activities when Paz resigned as ambassador in 1968, but even as late as 1975 he was writing of Elena and his daughter to his close friend and publisher in Spain, Pere Gimferrer of Elena:

They are now in Madrid, and from there, as always, I can hear the furious buzz of those two enraged bees. Whenever they get the opportunity, they plant their poisoned sting into me, and are constantly plotting and slandering in order to blackmail me, get money out of me, ruin me and shame me . . . It's dreadful to feel yourself hated.[25]

In June 1959, Paz left his home country yet again, this time bound for Paris as first secretary in the Mexican embassy.[26] Bona by now was divorced from Pieyre de Mandiargues, and the couple rented an apartment from the widow of the Surrealist poet Paul Eluard. Describing a visit to the household, a Peruvian friend José Durand recalls not only how happy Paz seemed to be back in Paris, but how intrigued he was by experimental kinds of poetry:

> We found him listening to recordings of electronic and concrete music (Varèse and co.). Having recorded this onto magnetic tape, OP is patiently trying to edit the words of a poem with the music. He said he wanted to bring together music and poetry, as he recalled from the works of the ancient Provencal artists. While he is doing this, his wife Bona is painting canvases and some suggestive collages; he is sitting on the floor, working away with a tape recorder, tapes, a pair of scissors, glue.[27]

This time, Paz's stay in Paris lasted only three years. He renewed his friendship with his Surrealist friends André Breton and Benjamin Péret, collaborating with them on the *Almanaque surréaliste du demi-siècle*, as part of the movement's big 1959 exhibition. He also made a new friend in Georges Bataille, the writer and intellectual who, like the Mexican author, was deeply interested in desire and the problem of evil in history. In general, though, Paz seems to have been less involved in the intellectual life of the French capital, where the Fourth Republic had just collapsed, and General de Gaulle had returned to create the Fifth Republic in his own image. Instead, Paz seemed content to explore his newfound personal happiness, and it seems to have been his wish to live this new life in fresh surroundings, which in 1962 led him to accept an offer to become Mexican ambassador to India. His hope was to persuade Bona to join him, so that they could live this new adventure together. Before leaving France he published another short collection of poems, *Salamandra*

('Salamander').[28] One of the first poems, 'Noche en claro' ('Clear Night') is a homage to Breton and Péret, and also to Bona and Paris itself:

> *La ciudad se despliega*
> *Su rostro es el rostro de mi amor*
> *Sus piernas son piernas de mujer*
> *Torres plazas columnas puentes calles*
> *Río cinturón de paisajes ahogados*
> *Ciudad o Mujer Presencia*

> The city unfolds
> Its face is the face of my love
> Its legs are a woman's legs
> Towers squares columns bridges streets
> river belt of drowned landscapes
> City or Woman Presence

As well as some typically exuberant Surrealist imagery, the poem contains more experimentation with typography (it includes the drawing of a hand), and other formal innovations. As Paz told the Spanish writer Julián Ríos in 1973: 'In *Salamandra* the plurality of voices/spaces/times is accentuated. In this book there is a short poem in which one line corresponds to text A, the next to text B, and so on. The result is that the poem is made up of three texts: A, B, and the union of these two: C.'[29] Elsewhere there is a quotation from the Chinese book of prophecy the *I Ching,* which Paz consulted often in these years, seeing in it another way in which past and future are gathered in the present moment. Jason Wilson notes that the whole collection bears evidence of his close attention to the works of the two earlier French poets, Apollinaire and Stéphane Mallarmé, and their attempts to free the text of poems from linear progression, often isolating words on the white page, while on the other freeing those poetic words from all the accretions that everyday usage has given them: in Mallarmé's famous phrase, 'purifying the language of the tribe'.[30]

As the later poems of *Salamandra* and, in particular, the title poem suggest, although the erotic union with a woman was still the key to the world of poetic revelation, the possibility of fusing one existence with another remained an inherently fleeting epiphany: by definition, it seemed, love destroyed itself through its own intensity. In 1962 Bona came out to India, and the two travelled extensively in the region (part of Paz's mission was to establish relations between Mexico and the newly independent Sri Lanka and Afghanistan). However, the adventure did not last: it was not long before Bona returned to France, where she eventually remarried Pieyre de Mandiargues.

In India alone, Paz sought solace in more travel. As he wrote to the French writer Claire Céa, whose introduction to his work appeared in the influential 'Poètes d'aujourd'hui' series published in Paris: 'I like landscapes and the people who are part of them (nomads, fishermen, mountain-dwellers), but I also like big cities. Last year [1963] I travelled a lot, and the more I discover countries and places, the thirstier I become for more.' His letter to the French editor then blossoms, as so often in Paz's writing, into a graphic description of what has been going on his mind during these journeys of discovery:

My attempts to think, and the few moments of revelation I have experienced are in what I have written – a slender work: I am not a literary professional and besides, I am incapable of a sustained effort . . . I write to know the world and to know myself – and also to invent myself. But above all, I write to prolong the lived experience – not to render it eternal, but to make it more intense and to make the unique instant that is the lived instant more lucid . . . not eternity, la vivacité, liveliness.[31]

Soon afterwards, in the sort of unexpected encounter that Breton and the Surrealists put so much faith in, Paz's life took another abrupt change of direction. This was when he met Marie-José Tramini, then married to a French diplomat. The couple were married in 1966, 'under a giant *nim* tree'. At 50, Paz had found a love that seemed natural and inevitable:

Me crucé con una muchacha . . .
Nuestros cuerpos
Se hablaron, se juntaron y se fueron.
Nosotros nos fuimos con ellos . . . [32]

I met a young girl . . .
Our bodies
Spoke together, got together, and left.
We left with them . . .

Paz's official duties in India were not especially onerous. He received visits from many old friends, including Henri Michaux and the Argentine writer Julio Cortázar, who had written approvingly of his work since the mid-1940s in the influential Argentine magazine *Sur*. As well as a fascination with France and French culture, the two men shared many literary interests: an enjoyment of the ludic side of language as well as a wish to renew literary language, a fascination with chance and an interest in the mysterious unpredictability of life. Paz in fact once told the Spanish writer Julián Ríos that the Argentine writer was the person he felt closest to in spirit of all his contemporaries. [33] Increasingly, even though he was based in India, Paz began to receive invitations to read his poetry or to give lectures in many parts of the world, including the United States. There he made new artistic friends, such as the American composer John Cage, whose musical work was frequently concerned with time, silence and chance in similar ways to Paz's approach to poetic language in these years. In fact, it is John Cage in his book of essays *A Year from Monday* who includes this wry comment from Paz on the duties of his ambassadorial post in India:

> I asked Paz whether being a diplomat took
>   Too much time from his poetry.   He said
> It didn't.   'There is no trade between the
>   Two countries.   They are on the very
>   Best of relations.'[34]

His travels and his new wife helped infuse Paz with an energy and optimism that was to lead to another important collection of poems that deal with his experiences in India, *Ladera este*.[35] Paz was also writing about the work of other poets from the Western tradition. This book of essays, *Cuadrivio*, was published in 1965.[36] In it he takes a lengthy look at the work of four of his favourite poets: Fernando Pessoa, whose work he had translated, and whose experiments with four entirely different poetic voices chimed in with his own experimental concerns in the early 1960s; Rubén Dario, the founder of modern poetry in Latin America; the Mexican poet Ramón López Velarde, who like Paz had been fascinated by Japanese poetry, and his old friend from the days of the Spanish Republic, Luis Cernuda.

At the same time, influenced by the work of the French poet Stéphane Mallarmé, Paz continued to wrestle with new ways of presenting his poetry. In 1965 he published *Blanco*: in its original edition, it unfolded in one long pleated cascade, with different coloured inks denoting different voices inside the text.[37] Paz told the Spanish writer Julián Ríos how it might be read:

> The text can be split into two, to form two independent poems, while the second of these can be read as four separate texts or as two; and finally, the whole poem can be read as fourteen isolated

poems. Corresponding to this syntactic rotation is a semantic rotation. And yet the poem is always the same poem: what is signified changes, but the meaning does not. That is why the poem is called 'Blanco'. The text travels from the blank page (what has not been written, the silence before speech) to the target (silence after speech), and on its way passes through four colours, four elements, four variations of sensation, perception, imagination and understanding. The fixed centre of the poem is also the target: the desired object.[38]

A further insight into Paz's intention in writing *Blanco* comes from his discussion of its translation with the English poet Charles Tomlinson, whom he met at the Spoleto and London International Poetry Festivals in 1967. Debating what might be the best English translation of the title, Tomlinson suggested (in a letter of March 1968) that 'The White Centre' might be a good way of implying its variety of meanings. In response, Paz wrote one of his typically intense expositions, suggesting that perhaps the word 'cipher' came closest to the original:

> I read in the dictionary: '*Cipher* (cipher). –From the Arab si'/ar. The character o – a nonety- a secret mode of writing'. And in *Buddhism*, by E. Conze: 'The little circle which we know as zero, was known to the Arabs about 950 A.D. as *shifr*, empty. In English we had originally *cypher* as the name of zero' (the English took it from the Spanish) 'and cipher is nothing but the Sanskrit word *sunya*'. Well, the original title of *Blanco* (which I rejected for obvious reasons) was Sunya or Sunyata . . . *Sunya* is always target, unreachable goal. So here is my question: does the word Cipher, with its additional meaning of 'secret writing' express any of all this? Or do you think it would be better as *Blank/Centre/White*?[39]

Paz's manuscript of *Blanco*, 1969.

Blanco is also an intensely erotic poem, as the Tantric Buddhist
epigraph (together with one from Mallarmé) suggests. In it the
outside world is reduced to the figure of a poet in a room listening
to music playing and the sounds of a woman close by him: the act
of writing and the act of love-making become one and the same.
The reader also partakes of this movement of liberation through
passion by the recreation of the moment; by interpreting the black
signs on the white of the page he or she makes the opposite journey to that of the poet. The two meet in the 'unreachable goal' of

the imminent present symbolized by the white of the page, the paroxysm of ecstatic love.

The poem was included in Paz's collection from his years in India, *Ladera este*. There is a new, much happier, tone to these poems, one of which is simply entitled 'Felicidad en Herat' ('Happiness in Herat'). In part this was due to his new companion, Marie-José. But it was also due to his prolonged immersion in an ancient, non-Western culture that reminded him of Mexico, despite its huge differences. His discovery of Buddhism and its reflections on time, the search for the here and now, and its transcendence of the routine flow of time, also fascinated him. Unlike *Blanco*, many of the other poems in the collection are direct impressions of the outside world, with the teeming life of Indian cities vividly described, the lines of the poem evoking movement, transience, details grasped in the rushing flow of time. Perhaps the most convincing expression of his poetic preoccupations at this time comes in 'Vrindaban'. Once again, the poem opens with the figure of a poet writing at night, and leads from memories of childhood to the more recent sights and sounds of India. The act of remembering and the act of writing propel him into the present moment, and induce him to seek out the meaning of what he has been and what he is now. The image of an Indian holy man offers him wisdom, but the poet has to reject answers found by anyone else, however wise: all he can count on are his own perceptions and intuitions:

> *Yo estoy en la hora inestable*
> *El coche corre entre las casas*
> *Yo escribo a la luz de una lámpara*
> *Los absolutos las eternidades*
> *Y sus aledaños*
> > *no son mi tema*
> *Tengo hambre de vida y también de morir*

Sé lo que creo y lo escribo
Advenimiento del instante

I am in the unstable hour
The car races between houses
I write by lamplight
Absolutes, eternities
And their vicinities
                  are not my theme
I am hungry for life and for dying
I know what I believe and write it
Advent of the instant.[40]

In addition to the poems written in India, Paz was equally prolific in his writing about poetry. He wrote *Los signos en rotación* and on the emerging fashion of structuralism. This was his 'Claude Lévi-Strauss o el nuevo festín de Esopo' ('Claude Lévi-Strauss or Aesop's New Feast'). This is Paz's most passionate defence of poetry. He considers Lévi-Strauss to have unfairly dismissed it in comparison to music or myth, and reasserts its ability to transcend time and create something truly new and original.

However, as on previous occasions, this settled period of Paz's life came to an abrupt end. In 1968 Paz followed the 'May events' in Paris and the anti-Vietnam protests in the United States with great interest. In common with many others he celebrated what appeared to be the almost Surrealist attitude to freedom made evident in the slogans of the young demonstrators on the streets of the French capital: 'L'imagination au pouvoir', 'défense de défendre' and so on. He also applauded the youthful protestors for the way in which they sought to throw off left-wing orthodoxy: their revolt in many ways seemed to him like a return to the spontaneous rebellion he had so greatly admired in Republican Spain in his younger days.

That same summer there were massive demonstrations in Mexico. The PRI regime, now headed by President Gustavo Díaz Ordaz, wanted to show the world that Mexico was capable of holding the xixth Olympic Games in Mexico City. When students began to protest that this was a huge waste of money in a country as poor as Mexico, with banners reading: 'Libros sí, bayonetas no!' or 'los agitadores: ignorancia, hambe, y miseria', their marches were brutally repressed by the police. President Díaz Ordaz was convinced it was all part of a plot hatched in Cuba to undermine the Games, and had tanks stationed around the university campus. This only brought more students and sympathizers out onto the streets of the capital, and led to further violence: part of Paz's beloved San Ildefonso College was destroyed. By the end of September there was a tense standoff between the two sides. The student leaders called a huge meeting in the Plaza de las tres culturas in Tlatelolco, in the north of the city. The three cultures were represented by an Aztec temple, one of the first churches from the Spanish colonial era, and the massive 1950s housing complex of Nonoalco-Tlaltelolco, which ironically contained the huge marble-clad modern building of the Mexican Foreign Ministry: Paz's employers.[41]

The student meeting was due to be held at 5 pm on 2 October. About 10,000 students and their supporters gathered in the square. Armoured cars took up positions around it; and at a certain moment, the shooting started. It has never been properly established who fired first: the police and army units claimed they were responding to being shot at, while the student leaders always maintained that at a prearranged signal the security forces simply fired into the crowd. Nor does anyone know for certain how many people died: the official death toll was between 20 and 40, the student leaders claimed it was more than 150, while in Britain the *Guardian* newspaper spoke of 325 people being shot or crushed to death in the stampede to get out of the line of fire.

In India, Paz listened horrified to the news on his radio. His decision to offer his resignation was immediate. As Guillermo Sheridan has pointed out, the conditions of his employment as ambassador meant that he could not in fact resign, but he was withdrawn from his post as ambassador and placed 'at the disposition' of the Mexican president for three years.[42] On the day after the massacre he wrote an indignant poem to the organizers of the cultural activities surrounding the Olympic Games, who had previously invited him to join in a 'Poetry Olympics' as part of the celebrations. The short verses alternate a description of the efforts to clean the blood from the square with the expression of his indignation and horror. He concludes with a warning:

La verguenza es ira
Vuelta contra uno mismo:
                    Si
Una nación entera se averguenza
Es león que se agazapa
Para saltar

Shame is anger
Turned against oneself
                    If
An entire nation feels ashamed
It is a lion crouching
Ready to leap [43]

Paz and his wife left India at the end of October, bound for Spain. In Mexico, the official press began a vicious campaign against him, claiming that he had in fact been dismissed from his post before he had resigned, because of making inappropriate comments. Perhaps the unkindest cut came from declarations by his former wife Elena

Garro and their daughter, claiming that by siding with the students, Paz was encouraging terrorism.[44]

A year later, in 1969, in what began as a lecture to the University of Texas in Austin, Paz delivered his verdict on the massacre. This was eventually expanded into a book, *Postdata* (translated as *The Other Mexico*) that was included in subsequent editions of *El laberinto de la soledad*.[45] In *Posdata*, Paz once more stresses the duty of the writer and intellectual to adopt a critical attitude towards history, and not to be blinded by any ideology. He goes on to criticize the Mexican political system for being undemocratic, and allowing the original revolutionary spirit to be lost in bureaucracy, institutional-ization and the worship of power. Because of the lack of a critical viewpoint, time repeats itself in a cyclical way, with the PRI present tragically echoing the Aztec past. He writes: 'It's no accident that those young people of Mexico fell in the ancient square of Tlatelolco: that was where the Aztec temple was situated, and where they practiced human sacrifice . . . in 1968, the aim was to spread terror among the people, using the same methods of human sacrifice as the Aztecs had employed.' His attack on the PRI government and its monolithic 'pyramid' of power made him a hero to many in Mexico. But his refusal to go beyond this criticism and call for a new revolu-tion also meant that the most radical elements among the students felt that he was not on their side. This placed Paz in an uncomfort-able position in the middle of two antagonistic groups: in the years that followed, he was to insist that this liberal, critical, middle way was right not merely for him, but for Mexico and the rest of Latin America as well. His belief in revolution was left far in the past, as he put his faith in lucid argument and the rejection of all ideology. Positive change comes about not through mass revolution, but through private dedication and the fleeting revelation of life's possibilities in works of poetry.

5

Bringing it all Back Home, 1969–90

The political situation in Mexico after the Tlatelolco killings was chaotic. Many of the 1968 student leaders had been hauled away, tortured and then sent to Lecumberri prison in the centre of Mexico City on entirely trumped-up charges. (Most of them were released thanks to a presidential amnesty in 1971.) But President Díaz Ordaz declared the Olympic Games a huge success, and in his memoirs claimed to have saved Mexico from 'the Communist menace': 'They wanted to change this Mexico of ours; they want to change it for a different one, one we do not like. If we want to keep our Mexico and if we stay united, they will not succeed.'[1] In 1970 he handed presidential power to the man who had been his Interior Minister at the time, Luis Echeverría. Both of these men orchestrated smear campaigns against Octavio Paz, claiming that his support for the striking students showed he was trying to overthrow the PRI regime in favour of a Marxist revolution.

Those on the left who were pressing for radical change in Mexico, however, seemed to have understood Paz's political position more accurately. They saw that his criticism of the PRI regime stopped well short of a call for revolution. In consequence, they too attacked the poet: in their view his liberal stance was a betrayal of what their movement stood for. Not for the first time, Paz found himself in an uncomfortable position in the middle. In 1969 he preferred to keep his distance, and accepted several of the many offers he received to become poetry professor at internationally known

Paz, mid-1970s.

institutions: first at the University of Texas, then for a year as Simon Bolivar professor at the University of Cambridge in England.

In addition to lecturing about his views on poetry – soon to be collected in *Los hijos del limo* (translated as 'Sons of the Mire'),[2] Paz used the time to reflect on what his years in India had brought him. These thoughts were gathered most memorably in the long prose poem *El mono gramático* ('The Monkey Grammarian').[3] *The Monkey Grammarian*[4] was written for the series Sentiers de la Création, brought out by the art publishers Skira in Geneva. The series was intended to combine illustrations and text, and the brief was for poets to shed some light on how they came to write – others who wrote for the series were mostly French poets, such as Yves Bonnefoy or René Char. As Paz says in his own book, he took the

Hanuman, the Monkey Grammarian and messenger of the gods in the Hindu *Ramayana*.

title of the series literally, and immediately started thinking of the poetic process as a journey. On one level this was the journey of memory. This took him back to India and the ruined holy city of Galta, which he had visited with Marie-José early in their marriage. The temples of Galta were mainly dedicated to Hanuman, the monkey messenger of the gods in the Hindu tradition, and the city itself when the couple visited it was over-run by monkeys. The ruins of Galta, writes Paz, remind him of how language's attempts to seize the present are almost always doomed to failure – the poet is merely seizing on the ruins of past meaning. And yet the poet's task is an essential one: Paz chooses Hanuman as his tutelary deity because, as a preliminary note informs us, in the *Ramayana* the monkey was seen as a grammarian, using language to criticize the gods.

But the creative journey also starts from the figure of the poet in the moment of the present, sitting at his desk in the twilight in Churchill College, Cambridge, scrutinizing the world around him and trying to seize what that moment has to offer. This perception leads Paz to ask himself what inner journey he is embarking on when he, like Hanuman, tries to use language as a poet. He believes that grammar is the critique of paradise, of all absolutes, and it is this that gives otherwise blank signs their meaning. The work of the poet is a paradoxical one. His task is to strip away this blankness, to deprive words of their usual meaning, 'undoing names' in order to get at what they really signify. As so often in Paz, the ability to truly name the world, while being immersed in the sensory assault that modern-day India implies for the senses, is offered only fleetingly. This leads Paz to consider how language can grasp the moment, can find fixity in the midst of the constant flux of the world and its phenomena. Sometimes there seems an almost mischievous, monkey-like delight in Paz's use of language as a philosophical dance: 'a tree is not the name tree, nor is it the sensation of a tree: it is the sensation of a perception of tree that dies away at the very moment of the perception of the sensation of tree'.[5] Here, as in much of his work of the period, Paz is acutely aware that language is a 'thicket of signs', only tenuously constructing meaning.

Two further constants of Paz's work come to the fore in *The Monkey Grammarian*: although there is no mention of it in the *Ramayana*, Paz gives Hanuman a female counterpart, known here as 'Splendor'. The sexual coupling with her provides the surest way to glimpse the longed-for moment of revelation. Second, as elsewhere in his work, writing and reading are here seen as two parts of the same journey, the mirror image of one another:

The transmutation of forms and their changes and movements into motionless signs: writing; the dissipation of the signs: reading. Through writing we abolish things, we turn them into meaning; through reading, we abolish signs, we extract the meaning from them, and almost immediately thereafter, we dissipate it: the meaning returns to the primordial stuff.[6]

Just prior to *The Monkey Grammarian*, Paz published two short collections which showed that he was continuing to broaden his experiments with poetic form, as another way of trying to arrive at the uniqueness of poetic expression. *Discos Visuales* ('Visual Discs'), published in 1968, consisted of two discs that the reader has to rotate in order to glimpse text fixed on the bottom disc.[7] *Topoemas*, which first appeared in 1971, consists of calligrams with words in his own handwriting, plays on words and their possible meanings, the shapes of texts on the white of the page.[8] Here again Paz is questioning the links between words as signs and as objects, the oscillation between the reality of the physical world and that of thought and language, the constructors of meaning. He has described them as a 'recourse against discourse': attempts to break down the inevitable development of an argument within a text, however poetic, an invitation to the reader to pause and contemplate the physicality of each word as sign.

Then, in the spring of 1969, when he was spending several weeks in Paris, he embarked on the experience of poetry written with others, as André Breton, Philippe Soupault, Paul Eluard and others had done in the early, heroic days of Surrealism in the 1920s. The other collaborators on what in 1971 became the book *Renga* were the English poet Charles Tomlinson, the French poet Jacques Roubaud and the Italian Edoardo Ungaretti.[9] The four men shut themselves up in the Hotel Saint-Simon in Paris, where they attempted to recreate the Japanese *renga* form of collaborative poetry written in a chain. The poets' aim was to produce four groups of seven sonnets, with each writer contributing four lines of each sonnet and translating the whole work into his own language. In the end Ungaretti pulled out and never translated the texts or wrote his final contributions. Although one of the aims of the experiment was to see if the poets' identities dissolved when faced with the formal constraints they imposed on themselves, the final result often reads like a pastiche of their own work.

Paz was to continue this kind of collaborative venture with Charles Tomlinson, who was also a skilled translator of his work. The two men exchanged airmail poems (sonnets once more) based on the themes of Day and House. As in *Renga*, each sonnet was divided into four sections, with each poet taking his turn. The exchange, which is above all a celebration of friendship – and on Tomlinson's side at least, of the existence of the real world outside – was published as *Hijos del aire* ('Airborn') in 1981.[10]

In the end, it was not until late 1971 that Paz returned to live in Mexico, although his international reputation meant that from now on he travelled abroad even more frequently than previously. This time he came back to Mexico City to help found a new maga-zine, *Plural*, that was published as a monthly literary supplement to the newspaper *Excélsior*. The newspaper editor, Julio Scherer García, was one of those who thought that the events of 1968 showed the desperate need for change in the Mexican political sys-tem; his newspaper was openly critical of party and president. Paz shared his view of the one-party state run by the PRI: 'In Mexico there is no other dictatorship besides that of the PRI, and there is no threat of anarchy apart from that brought about by the unnatu-ral prolongation of its political monopoly', he wrote.[11] Paz made *Plural* the standard-bearer for liberal democratic opinions, as its name suggests, insisting that political and cultural change could only come about through the free exercise of rational criticism – something that he considered had passed Mexico and the rest of Latin America by as a result of eighteenth-century's Spain's rejec-tion of the Enlightenment and its values. The first issue included contributions by his old Argentine friends Jorge Luis Borges and Adolfo Bioy Casares and, as in all his previous magazines, Paz strove to make *Plural* a conduit for international voices and trends.

During his six years in office, President Luis Echeverría made determined attempts to convince Mexico's leading intellectuals that

The cover of *Plural*, 1961.

he was progressive, while at the same time insisting that he wanted to return to the real roots of the Mexican revolution and finish a job started some sixty years earlier. Paz was one of those who could not at this time see the PRI reforming into a modern democratic party, and in response helped found the Comité nacional de auscultación y consulta (CNAC) (National Committee for Examination and Consulting), which eventually became the left-wing Partido Mexicano de los Trabajadores (Mexican Workers' Party).[12] Paz withdrew soon after the committee's creation, judging that what Mexico most needed was a group of independent observers rather than direct political involvement. As he told an interviewer some years later: 'When I came back in the 1950s, the important thing was to give

expression to Mexico. When I came back in the 1970s, the fundamental thing was to reflect on Mexico with a view to changing it.'[13]

As well as reflecting on his home country, Paz continued to
publish his thoughts about poetry and its importance. His experiences as a translator from many languages and his reflections on
translation were collected in a book.[14] The lectures he had given at
Harvard in 1971–2 were amplified for publication in 1974 as *Los
hijos del limo* ('Sons of the Mire').[15] In many ways this is a continuation of his questioning of the value of poetry first explored in detail
in *El arco y la lira*. In the new text Paz once more compares and
contrasts poetic and religious revelation, as well as the temptation
of poetry proclaiming a revolution in language and in life. Modern
poetry, Paz argues, seeks to get beyond representation to reality
itself. But in so doing it becomes its own negation; as José Quiroga
writes in *Understanding Octavio Paz*: 'the modern poem works by
means of a negative operation: it can only be a text by denying
itself as a poem, and it erects that very same negation as the fundamental point of origin for its own song. The more absolute the
sense of negation is, the more is a space opened.'[16]

This view of the goal of modern poetry shows how Mallarmé
and his search for absolutes are still crucial to the Mexican poet.
This, too, is at the heart of the long poem Paz published in 1974,
Pasado en claro (translated as 'A Draft of Shadows').[17] In interview
the poet described this as an attempt to look back at his childhood
and early adolescence in order to discover 'the seed of the man I
was to become'. Once again this is a moral quest, as Paz claims
that 'what is important in every human life is to be worthy of the
child we once were'.[18] At the same time, however, *Pasado en claro*
goes beyond any anecdotal intention to ask the question of how
language as a system of signs can both uncover and express the
reality of which it is part. Can it stand outside that reality and
offer the poet and his reader the possibility to get to know that
reality in a significant and unique way?

A traves de nosotros habla consigo mismo
El universo. Somos un fragmento
– pero cabal en su inacabamiento –
de su discurso. Solipsismo
coherente y vacío:
desde el principio del principio
¿Qué dice? Dice que nos dice.
Se lo dice a si mismo.

Through us the universe
talks to itself. We are a fragment
– complete in its incompleteness –
of its discourse. A coherent
and empty solipsism:
from the beginning of the beginning
What does it say? It says it says
Us.
It says it to itself.[19]

As well as *Pasado en claro*, Paz gathered the other poems he had
written since his abrupt departure from India in the collection *Vuelta*
('Return'),[20] first brought out in 1976. This title and its choice for the
magazine he was to set up in 1977 show his determination to make
this return to his home country a definitive one: he and his new wife,
who was living in Mexico for the first time, were here to stay. These
poems are a re-examination of his own life and past, a more personal
slant on the kind of questioning of Mexico, its recent history and
possibilities for the future, that he was undertaking in his journalism
and other public utterances. 'Vuelta' is also the title of a single poem,
written soon after his reinsertion into the maelstrom of Mexico City.
In the poem, as in the collection as a whole, Paz contrasts the 'sub-
verted Eden' of contemporary Mexico with the sustaining images of
his past. Now it is not the toad of 'El cántaro roto' who is master, but

the vultures and coyotes who rule over this 'heap of broken words'. But, as in *The Monkey Grammarian*, it is thanks to a moment's revelation in the darkness of night that the poet is able still to affirm the value of life despite all the horrors of twentieth-century history. 'Nocturno de San Ildefonso' begins with him back in 1931, when he was attending San Ildefonso College, and the year he published his first poem. It is also a reflection on the distance travelled since his previous poem about return to Mexico in 'Piedra de sol', written 20 years earlier. As in that poem, the beginning and end reflect each other, in a spiral, circular movement. 'Nocturno' moves from looking out onto and imagining the city outside, to a consideration of his own life and that of his friends and contemporaries: 'El bien, quisimos el bien/ enderezar el mundo/ No nos faltó entereza: / nos faltó humildad', 'Good, it was good we wanted/ to set the world to rights. We did not lack integrity /it was humility we lacked'. It goes on to a more general reflection on how these youthful dreams of justice foundered on the dry rocks of history, before returning to the moment of the poem's creation, which brings with it the affirmation of life brought about by the knowledge that his wife is asleep nearby as the night turns into a new day, the 'fluir sosegado', 'peaceful flow' of her breathing reassuring the poet and validating his efforts.

The battle with outside reality suggested in 'Nocturne de San Ildefonso' was never more evident than in 1976, when the Echeverría government sent soldiers to close down *Excélsior* and forced the editor, Julio Scherer García, to resign. As in 1968 Paz had no hesitation in following suit, resigning from his post as editor of *Plural*, and taking the whole of the staff with him. A year later he began his own independent magazine, *Vuelta*, which over the years to come was to provide a critical, liberal voice inside Mexico, while at the same time bringing new literature and ideas from many countries into the Mexican intellectual scene. In both the magazines he headed in the 1970s and 1980s Paz sought to defend the importance of art and literature both for its own sake and for the counterweight it provided to political power because of its independence. He also increasingly saw the magazine as a counterweight to what he saw as the hegemony of the Marxist left in Mexican universities, particularly the autonomous state university, UNAM: his own alma mater. As André Breton had done in France, Paz fiercely defended the figure of the free-spirited intellectual who refused to be part of either the political establishment or the university elite. He criticized the growing influence of new disciplines such as sociology and political science, insisting on the more traditional idea of the 'man of letters' who could express his opinion on all topics without having studied any one specific area.[21]

After 1968 some radical academics and students argued that the moment was ripe for another revolution in Mexico. Various groups took to the mountains of Guerrero and other states in an attempt to replicate the Cuban revolution and the idea of the revolutionary 'foco' which would spread revolution from the countryside to the cities. In the pages of his magazines, and in numerous public speeches, Paz argued that there was no room for violent revolution in the Mexico of the 1970s. In his view, this would only make the dominant PRI party all the more authoritarian. Instead, he and his colleagues urged a reform of the Mexican state from within, pushing the PRI to become more democratic and opening spaces for a greater number of Mexican citizens. This view of the Mexican state formed the basis for another collection of essays, *El ogro filantrópico* ('The Philanthropic Ogre'),[22] which continued his investigation of the 'meaning' of Mexican history and the Mexican state after the revolution. In addition the book continues his criticism of political systems (principally 'scientific' Marxism) which view history as a straight line of progress towards a future utopia. As ever, Paz argues in favour of dissidence, singularity, of a more immediate assertion of liberty through a personal, moral revolt against oppression.

In 1979 Paz published his collected poems, under the title *Poemas*

1935–1975.[23] As in previous collections, he took the opportunity to suppress poems he no longer felt he could identify with (including all his youthful efforts), as well as reordering and updating others. To some extent, this redefinition of his past is a result of his increasing concern with personal and historic memory; it also seems like the work of someone who feels he is embattled, seeking to define and defend his position in a hostile environment.

The distance between Paz and the Mexican left was further exacerbated by his sustained criticism of the Soviet Union and other socialist countries. In his magazines and in public he condemned the Soviet system as totalitarian in a way that Mexico was not. But his critics on the left accused him and his colleagues of wittingly or unwittingly being champions of the right, and of failing to condemn the rise of the extreme right in Latin America, with the overthrow of President Allende's 'peaceful road to socialism' in Chile in 1973, or the installation of military dictatorships in Argentina, Brazil and Uruguay. The ferocity and personal nature of these arguments has led many commentators on Paz to see his next major work, the lengthy, brilliant biography on the seventeenth-century Mexican nun and writer Sor Juana Inés de la Cruz, published in 1982,[24] as in part a self-defence.[25] Sor Juana was a figure who had fascinated Paz since the 1940s: he wrote a long article on her for the Argentine magazine *Sur* published in 1951, and returns to her in his *El laberinto de la soledad*. For Paz, the nun who was forced to give up her writing because of the forces of the establishment – in her day, the Catholic Church and the Inquisition – was another example of the individual creative artist who cannot find support or sympathy in the society around them. He draws a direct parallel between her situation and that of the second half of the twentieth century: 'The intellectual history of orthodoxies – whether it is that of the Counter-Reform in Spain or that of Marxist-Leninism in Russia – is the story of the mummification of knowledge.'[26]

Paz is fascinated by many questions thrown up by the figure of the first Mexican female poet, praised as the 'tenth muse': what made Sor Juana become a nun? What kind of a society had Spain created in Mexico by the end of the seventeenth century? What were the forces at work on an individual in that strange hybrid society which directly shaped her work, since, as he argues: 'In every society a system of prohibitions and authorizations is at work . . . establishing what can and what cannot be said.'[27] And the main question: why did she give in to the Church authorities and accept not only silence, but abandon all attempts to read and learn, to curtail her intellectual curiosity? Together with *El laberinto de la soledad*, *Sor Juana* is Paz's most accomplished prose work. It is as though he were answering what he felt to be criticism from the 'academy' that he was an amateur (he had never completed his studies at university): the historical analysis of New Spain is rigorous and far less arbitrary than his previous historical forays; his appreciation of Sor Juana as a poet shows his deep knowledge of the Spanish Golden Age and of baroque poets; his views on the reasons for her silence are deeply felt and closely argued.

There can be no doubt that Paz felt himself under attack in similar ways during the 1980s in Mexico. He saw the Mexican intellectual orthodoxy as blindly following the tenets of Marxism, which he himself had rejected several decades earlier. He found himself vilified on many occasions, as when in 1980 he was denounced as being one of the theorists of the PIGS (Party of Intellectuals for Genocide): 'they are the shameless agents of the Club of Rome, the Brandt Commission and other planning and research centers of the Anglo-American oligarchy, whose aim is clear: to destroy Mexico's Republican institutions, and usher in a new dark age'. In response, he used his position as editor of *Vuelta*, his appearances on television and his international reputation, to propound his own liberal beliefs. Although during his years in the diplomatic service he had felt that Mexico's foreign policy was progressive and he had felt he could support it, in the 1980s he became increasingly critical of it. The Mexican government continued to enjoy friendly relations with Castro's Cuba, and was sympathetic to the guerrilla movements in El Salvador (even establishing relations with the Farabundo Martí Guerrilla Front) as well as with the Sandinista government which overthrew the Somoza dynasty in Nicaragua in 1979.

However, Paz was convinced that the solution to Latin America's problems lay through reform rather than revolution. He rejected the idea that representative democracy and its institutions were suitable for 'developed' countries such as those of Europe and the United States, but that the problems of less developed nations could only be solved by the violent overthrow of the national 'oligarchies'. In 1984, for example, when he was awarded the prestigious Peace Prize at the annual Frankfurt Book Fair, he took the opportunity to denounce the new regime in Nicaragua:

> The actions of the Sandinista government clearly show its desire to implant in Nicaragua a bureaucratic-military dictatorship following the model of Havana. Peace cannot be brought to Central America until the people of Nicaragua are allowed to express their opinion in genuinely free elections in which all parties are allowed to take part.[28]

Such was the revulsion caused by this speech among the left in Mexico, that in October of that year he had the dubious privilege of having his effigy burned during a protest demonstration of some 5,000 people outside the US embassy in Mexico City.

Paz's own views on the United States, as well as the Soviet Union, Western Europe and the Far East, were expounded in a book published in 1983, *Tiempo Nublado* ('Cloudy Weather').[29] As Enrique Krauze has pointed out, it is also a book aimed at Paz's left-wing critics, another attempt to explain his position to them and to attack what the poet sees as their blind dogmatism: 'Their forefathers swore by Saint Thomas, they swear by Marx, but for both of them reason is a weapon in the service of Truth with a capital letter. The intellectual's mission is to defend that truth. They have a polemical, combative view of culture and thought: they are crusaders.'[30] Although Paz perhaps could not see it, this is also an accurate description of his own attitude. Even though he was always respectful of the other person's opinion in any argument, he would not back down from telling the truth as he saw it, however unpalatable it might be to his audience. In 1987, for example, he returned to Valencia for the fiftieth anniversary of the anti-Fascist Congress that he had been part of during the Spanish Civil War. Once again he ruffled feathers by insisting that the Republicans admit they and their ideals were no longer something to aspire to: that the parliamentary democracy and constitutional monarchy of 1980s Spain were entirely legitimate.

This attitude made Paz an extremely controversial figure in 1980s Mexico, known more for his political opinions than for his poetry. Because he often appeared on the private television channel Televisa, which left-wing intellectuals denounced as a medium that gave a view of the world violently skewed to the right, he was frequently condemned out of hand. He himself continued to maintain that he was independent of all political forces, speaking out on subjects as his conscience demanded. But although he seemed to claim he was the victim in these arguments, his position as Mexico's leading intellectual gave him power and a platform frequently denied his adversaries. For example, he was able to write and present twelve programmes for Televisa which were later published as *México en la obra de Octavio Paz*,[31] an anthology of what he had written about the history, literature and artists of his home country.

As with his relations with the left, Paz's attitude to Mexico was never really resolved. Indeed, it is tempting to see his attitude to both as being very similar in kind to his reaction to his grandfather and father as reflected in the poem about them in *Ladera este*: they were the ones with the dramatic stories of violence and revolution

Paz appeared frequently – and often controversially – on Mexican TV in the 1970s and 1980s.

to tell, while his small voice of moderation could hardly be heard. He summed up these feelings in a July 1988 letter to his Catalan friend and publisher, Pere Gimferrer:

> We arrived eight days ago, and I still can't get used to Mexican reality. On neither the physical or the moral level. I still feel tired and also a vague sense of horror, an anguish that is hard to describe, but well-known and a part of me. It's a feeling I've had since childhood: what am I doing here? A perpetual *malentendu* poisons the relationship I have with my own people, especially with the writers, artists, and intellectuals, in other words, with all those who ought to be, if not my friends, at least my colleagues. I've written page upon page – more than two thousand of them – to try to dissipate this misunderstanding, but all in vain. Every time I return it's like starting all over again; every time I leave it's a flight. You can imagine what my state of mind is like. It is going to be hard to reconcile myself with my reality and to get back to work.[32]

Yet even now in his mid-seventies he was hard at work. In addition to his political articles, his television appearances, and his international commitments, he had time to produce what was to be his last volume of new poetry, *Árbol adentro* ('Tree Inside').[33] The collection is made up of five distinct sections. The first poems show the poet exploring inside himself and looking outside to the world in time. The second set of poems touch on friendship, and are dedicated to people Paz has felt close to over the years. The fourth part is also devoted to friends, but this time painters whom Paz has known and admired. The last part contains love poems, with woman as ever providing the main reason driving the poet to believe that his task is worthwhile. What is new is the third section, which reflects on the idea of death and is placed under the aegis of the French Renaissance philosopher and essayist Michel de Montaigne: 'to philosophize is to learn how to die'. Several poems, and in particular 'Ejercicio preparatorio (díptico con tablilla votiva)' ('Diptych with Votive Tablet'), are a rumination on how poetry can reconcile all elements of life in the face of its negation.

Two years later, in 1989, Paz was witness to a historic event which to him proved his political position had been right: the collapse of the Communist world in Eastern Europe, and the subsequent fall of the Soviet Union. He celebrated this in 'Pequeña crónica de grandes días' ('A Small Chronicle of Great Days').[34] Here he sees the collapse of the socialist world in Europe as the result both of a lack of legitimacy in power and the inability to compete economically with the West. At the same time, he does not regard the market as offering individual freedom in the way that Gustav Hayek or his intellectual supporters such as the Peruvian writer Mario Vargas Llosa (who was at that moment standing for the presidency of Peru on this libertarian ticket) argued. Instead, Paz proposed a recognition that both capitalism and socialism had something to offer mankind, but only if there was a recognition that the truth of genuine cultural expression also had a vital part to play in securing liberty for every individual.

In 1990 he also published *La otra voz: Poesía y fin de siglo*,[35] a book more directly concerned with poetry and its relation to history, particularly the idea of revolution and abrupt change, which he

Paz with his second wife, Marie-Jo, and, from left, Daniel Weissbort, Jason Wilson, Anthony Rudolf and Richard Burns – an academic and three poet-translators.

once again sees as a dead end. And in the same year, at the age of 76, Paz was awarded the Nobel Prize for Literature. The judges praised both his poetry and his prose, as well as his intellectual defence of freedom in all spheres. Paz responded in his acceptance speech with a discourse on the search for modernity in countries on the periphery like Mexico, and an insistence that the spiritual vacuum of the second half of the twentieth century must be filled if mankind was to remain true to its destiny.

6

Consuming Fires, 1990–98

The Nobel jury awarded Paz the literature prize for 'impassioned writing with wide horizons, characterized by sensual intelligence and humanistic integrity'. His acceptance speech embodies all these qualities.[1] He starts by pointing out that the languages of the Americas are 'transplanted tongues'; ones that have evolved to express a European reality, only to suddenly find themselves having to cope with an entirely different one. Not only that, Paz argues, but the Spanish conquest was unlike the Anglo-Saxon push into North America: in Mexico, for example, the Spaniards encountered 'history as well as geography'. Furthermore, Paz insists that this history is still alive: it is a present as much as a past. As a result, to be a Mexican writer in the twentieth century means to be aware of and to listen to that world which is still both present and presence. This awareness is what separates writers like him from the European tradition, he argues, and in consequence he suffers a double feeling of alienation: to the cultural is inevitably added the universal existential: the realization that each person is a separate consciousness, surrounded by a world that is irredeemably other. In a typical piece of Pazian lyricism, he then illustrates this abstract philosophical notion with an example from his own lived experience. He recalls his childhood home in Mixcoac, and the timeless paradise of its garden, with its mysterious huge fig tree, as well as the magical journeys offered by his grandfather's books.

But the time outside time of his childhood was bound to come to an end. Paz situates the moment when he realized this as when he

Paz signing books during his last visit to England in 1995.

saw illustrations in the newspaper of American troops returning from the First World War (when he must have been four or five). This was the moment when the outside world of history impinged directly on him; from then on time itself became something with which he had to reckon and struggle. Part of the struggle was his attempt to regain the eternal present glimpsed in his childhood, and this was the root of his desire to make poetry: 'poetry is in love with the instant and seeks to relive it in the poem, thus separating it from sequential time and turning it into a fixed present'.

In turn, this led him, Paz says, to seek 'modernity', in order to make his poetry speak to the world around him. Even though poetry is the search for the illuminating instant, it must also be intimately connected to the world outside if it is to fulfill its function as a spiritual quest. Here Paz's speech changes focus. As so often in these years, he criticizes the idea of modernity itself, which he calls a 'by-product of our conception of history as a unique and linear process of succession'. In this way, he moves from the poetic to the political, embodying in his speech the necessary connection between the two. The idea of history as a line heading towards ever greater progress has broken down in the twentieth century, he maintains, leaving us in a state of what he poetically terms 'the twilight of the future'.

He goes on to list what he sees as the reasons for this breakdown: mankind cannot go on believing in scientific or technological progress when the destructive forces they unleash have become so obvious; nor can man continue to use natural resources as if they were infinite without completely exhausting the planet. (This ecological concern increased the older Paz became, making him one of the first 'eco-warriors'.) Added to this, Paz argues, is the evidence from the twentieth century that mankind is not progressing on a spiritual level: millions of innocent victims have suffered 'slaughter, torture, humiliation, degradation'. This in itself has led to a widespread questioning of the need for progress if these are its consequences, as well as whether in fact there are any discernible laws in history.

The collapse of a belief in progress, concludes Paz, has left mankind 'in a sort of spiritual wilderness and not, as before, in the shadow of those religious and political systems that consoled us at the same time as they oppressed us'. From this idea, Paz returns to consider the moment, the present made even more crucial by this breakdown of any idea of progress towards a 'vague Utopia'. This brings him back to his starting point – why should not poetry be one of those 'pillars' which enables man to critically scrutinize the present: 'what do we know about the present? Nothing or almost nothing. Yet the poets do know one thing: the present is the source of presence', he concludes.

I have dwelt at length on Paz's Nobel speech because it is a good example of the kind of ideas that were preoccupying him as both poet and polemicist through much of his later life. His quest for poetic expression does not lead him away from the world; rather it is because the need for poetry is a moral imperative that he has constantly to measure its capacities against the reality beyond words on a page. After testing its claims, he can assert that poetry does offer 'real reality', one that is as magical as the world he lived in as a child, although in those days he had no need to express his sense of being in time. In its flowing argument Paz's Nobel speech mirrors the structure of many of his mature poems: the sense of a quest, the struggle with outside reality, the rejection of any utopia outside the moment of illumination. All that is missing here, perhaps out of a sense of *pudor*, is Paz's other main 'pillar' of belief: that of the ecstasy of sexual union as also providing a glimpse of this time outside time.

This exploration of sexuality is instead carried out at length in his last extended essay, *La llama doble* ('The Double Flame').[2] Paz himself said he had been writing the book for thirty years, since his researches into the work of the Marquis de Sade in the 1960s, and later when he was reading Charles Fourier. He completed it in an intense period of two months early in 1993, at the age of 79. The double flame of the title refers to the twin sources of eroticism and love: 'the original, primordial fire, sexuality, raises the red flame of eroticism, and this in turn raises and feeds another flame, tremulous and blue: the flame of love. Eroticism and love – the double flame of life.'[3] In his essay Paz revisits ideas about love and eroticism from Plato onwards to Arthur C. Clarke, roaming not only through the Western tradition, but drawing on his knowledge of that of India and the Far East. While praising eroticism as release from the mere animal instinct to reproduce, he goes on to define the difference between this force and love as essentially a question of freedom. Eroticism is the exercise of a person's imagination, but it is only in the choice of two people to surrender their own individual nature that love is born. Because each person fully chooses to be linked to the other, love is the ultimate respecter of freedom, and an affirmation of the individual human being. This, as Paz triumphantly states, means that 'love has been and is still the great act of subversion in the West'.[4]

Increasingly ill with heart problems (he had a multiple bypass operation in Texas in 1994) and other ailments, Paz continued to produce ambitious, sweeping essays that showed the breadth of his knowledge as well as being vividly autobiographical. In 1995, for example, he turned his mind back to India and all that he had learnt from it. As he had written in his book on Claude Lévi-Strauss: 'India is a giant cauldron, and he who falls in it can never get out'; now in *Vislumbres de la India* ('Glimpses of India') he wrote one of the first books in Spanish on the country, its history, society and culture.[5] During his time as ambassador there he had become very friendly with Indira Gandhi, and decided to put his impressions of India into book form on the tenth anniversary of her assassination. *Vislumbres* begins and ends with a 'cultural travelogue of India',[6] that is as vivid as the scenes described in the poems of *Ladera este* or *El mono gramático*, but the main chapters reflect on India's history and culture, comparing and contrasting them not only to Mexico, but to Western Europe and other civilizations in Asia. What particularly interests him is the way that India has somehow resisted Western notions of time and change – a resistance to change reflected in the caste system, which in his view prevents the idea of democracy truly taking hold. Paz also roams from classic poetry to religion to Indian cuisine. In all these aspects of its unique culture, Paz praises India's capacity to absorb outside influences and pressures while at the same time continuing to retain its distinctive identity – a situation he once more contrasts with the West, which he sees (as in the Nobel prize speech) as over-run by 'easy hedonism' and spiritual vacuity now that the myth of progress has disintegrated.

A few months after *La llama doble*, Paz published *Itinerario*,[7] which he called 'an intellectual biography but also a sentimental and even passionate one', since as he stresses, his work in poetry and prose had always sought to unite thought and feeling. As the title suggests, this is a description of what, from the vantage point of his 80 years, Paz sees as the significant stages on his political and spiritual journey. As with a lot of his writing at this time, it is once again an attempt to set the record straight before he dies. After reviewing his childhood passions, his struggles as a writer and a polemicist through the 1930s and since, he concludes sombrely that 'evil is human, exclusively human', and yet that does not lead him to despair. Instead, as ever, it arouses in him a desire to fight that evil.

Paz was also still fighting with a large part of Mexico's intelligentsia. While there was a great deal of official rejoicing that he was the first Mexican writer to win the Nobel Prize, his critics on the left saw it in ideological terms as a reward to the poet for his anti-Soviet stance in the year that the Berlin Wall fell and the Communist bloc was crumbling. Despite Paz's assertions that he was never an 'official' poet, there is little doubt that he was very close to the PRI in these years, especially under presidents Carlos Salinas de Gortari and his successor Ernesto Zedillo. Paz seemed convinced that these men were sincere in their attempts to democratize the all-powerful PRI, despite the widespread accusations that Salinas only won the 1988 election thanks to fraud, or the murder of the reformist candidate Donaldo Colosio prior to the 1994 elections which saw Zedillo take over the 'eagle's throne'.

Nor did Paz react enthusiastically to the Zapatista National Liberation Army (EZLN) uprising that took place on 1 January 1994 – the same day that Mexico entered its Free Trade Agreement with the United States and Canada. Many observers saw this as the proof – if any were needed – that Mexico at the end of the twentieth century

Paz's signature.

was just as divided as it had been at the start. In the same way that the dictator Porfirio Díaz had insisted that Mexico was a modern, progressive country when millions of poor peasants were working in near-slave conditions in much of the countryside, so now the Zapatistas and their masked leader Subcomandante Marcos drew attention to the fact that whilst the government was leading Mexico into ambitious free market deals, the indigenous peoples of the southern state of Chiapas and the rest of Mexico had been excluded from this supposed progress. As responsive to events going on around him as ever, Paz responded to the Zapatista uprising in two long articles published in the daily newspaper *La Jornada*.[8] While recognizing that the movement represented some legitimate claims of the indigenous populations of Mexico, he rejected the Zapatista's decision to pursue them through armed struggle, and went so far as to claim that the indigenous people were being manipulated by far-left groups.[9] Paz felt that their demands could and should be met through Mexico's democratic institutions, and not by demanding autonomy for indigenous areas, as this in his view would lead to the disintegration of the nation. He also dismissed the romantic appeal of Marcos: 'his strength is not reasoning, but emotion and unction: the pulpit and the mass rally'. As usual, beyond the indigenous groups and the Zapatistas, he was most indignant about the way that many Mexican intellectuals supported the EZLN without, in his view, thinking their position through.

Paz's combative attitude aroused his critics' ire still further. One of the most outspoken attacks on him in these last years came from a well-respected US academic and interpreter of Mexico, Ilan Stavans.[10] Reviewing Paz's work as an essayist, Stavans went so far as to call him a 'marionette of those in power', a 'tentacle of the state, a conformist who traded his dreams for institutional recognition', and even 'a cultural dictator undergoing his final decline'. Stavans even claimed to be writing on behalf of Mexican intellectuals who were uneasy about speaking up in Mexico for fear of reprisals.

Paz merely took this kind of vicious attack as further proof of the correctness of his view that 'orthodox' left-wing critics were narrow-minded, mean-spirited and shallow.

Far worse for him was the December 1996 fire that almost completely destroyed his apartment in the centre of Mexico City. Much of his collection of books was ruined, as was his invaluable collection of artefacts from Mexico, India, Japan and other nations. In addition, by now cancer had left him in a wheelchair and often in pain.

After the fire the Mexican authorities offered him an old house in Coyoacán in the south of the city to put his books, papers and collections in. This became the Octavio Paz Foundation, which he himself saw as a way of preserving his legacy. The house was reputed to be one of those built by Hernán Cortes during the Spanish invasion five centuries earlier. More recently it was the place where D. H. Lawrence had stayed in the early 1920s when he visited Mexico to gather material for his novel *The Plumed Serpent*: the superstitious Paz said he believed he could sense the spirit of the English writer still present in the old walls. The foundation was opened on 17 December 1997 in the presence of the Mexican president, Ernesto Zedillo; in giving his thanks Paz stressed how the true history of twentieth-century Mexico was the one written by its poets. He died a few months later on the evening of 19 April 1998. His final poem, appropriately enough a dialogue with the Spanish Golden Age poet Francisco de Quevedo, appeared in *Vuelta* in June 1998.[11] Part of it (in an English version by Eliot Weinberger) sums up many of his poetic concerns:

Por un instante, a veces, vemos
– no con los ojos: con el pensamiento –
Al tiempo reposar en una pausa
El mundo se entreabre y vislumbramos
El reino inmaculado
las formas puras, las presencias

The cover of the journal *Vuelta* commemorating Paz's death in 1998.

inmóviles flotando
sobre la hora, río detenido

For a moment, sometimes we see
– not with our eyes but with our thoughts –
time resting in a pause.
The world half-opens and we glimpse
the immaculate kingdom,
the pure forms, presences,
unmoving, floating
on the hour, a river stopped.

Unfortunately Paz did not live to see the year 2000 presidential elections, when the PRI was voted out of power without violence, and for the first time in more than seventy years Mexico experienced a change of political regime. Had he lived, Paz would undoubtedly have welcomed the change, and then almost immediately have begun to criticize its shortcomings.

References

1 Finding a Voice, 1914–37

1 Guillermo Sheridan, 'Paz en Paris: seis pasajes', *Cuadernos Hispanoamericanos*, DCLVIII (April 2005), pp. 21–32.
2 Octavio Paz, *La otra voz: Poesía y fin de siglo* (Barcelona, 1990), p. 55.
3 Octavio Paz, *Pasado en claro* (Mexico City, 1975), p. 29.
4 Octavio Paz, *Ladera este, Collected Poems 1957–1987* (Manchester, 1988), p. 222.
5 See Octavio Paz, *The Other Voice* (New York, 1991), pp. 143–60.
6 Paz, *Pasado en claro*, p. 28.
7 Octavio Paz, *Sor Juana: Her Life and Her World* (London, 1988).
8 Paz, *Pasado en claro*, p. 27.
9 Octavio Paz, *Itinerary*, trans. Jason Wilson (London, 1999), *passim*.
10 Ibid., pp. 101–10.
11 Octavio Paz, '¿Aguilo o Sol?', in *Libertad bajo Palabra* (Mexico City, 1960), p. 195.
12 Octavio Paz, *La hija de Rappaccini* (Mexico City, 1956).
13 Rita Guibert, *Seven Voices* (New York, 1973), p. 211.
14 Paz, *Itinerary*, pp. 18–20. However, in his *Poeta con paisaje: Ensayos sobre la vida de Octavio Paz* (Mexico City, 2004), the Mexican writer Guillermo Sheridan argues that Paz and his mother did not go to live with his father in California at this time (pp. 49–51). For Sheridan, in his old age Paz invented this 'false memory' as compensation for the lack of being with his father for much of his infancy.
15 Paz, *Itinerary*, p. 19.
16 Ibid., pp. 9–20.
17 Paz, *Pasado en claro*, p. 36.

18 Paz, *Itinerary*, p. 104.

19 Guibert, *Seven Voices*, p. 212.

20 Sheridan, 'Paz en Paris', p. 102.

21 Paz, *Itinerary*, p. 42.

22 See Sheridan, 'Paz en Paris', p. 172.

23 In Anthony Stanton, *Las primeras voces del poeta Octavio Paz (1931–1938)* (Mexico City, 2001), pp. 22–3.

24 Sheridan, 'Paz en Paris', p. 23.

25 Octavio Paz, *Al Paso*, p. 17.

26 Paz, *La otra voz*, pp. 55–70.

27 See Rafael Argullol, 'Poesía y enigma', *Insula*, 532–3 ([Madrid] April–May 1991) on Octavio Paz; Enrico Mario Santí, *Primeras Palabras sobre Primeras Letras* ([Madrid] April–May 1991), pp. 5–6.

28 Stanton, *Las primeras voces*, pp. 18–19.

29 Quoted in Héctor de Mauleón, 'Cartas de amor de Octavio Paz', *Confabulario*, cultural supplement of *El Universal de Mexico* (24 April 2004).

30 Octavio Paz, *Luna Silvestre* (Mexico City, 1933).

31 Paz, *Pasado en claro*, p. 29.

32 Octavio Paz, *No pasarán* (Mexico City, 1936).

33 Paz, *No pasarán*, p. 8.

34 Revised edition 1942, in *A la orilla del mundo* (Mexico City, 1942).

35 Paz, *La otra voz*, pp. 11–30.

36 Octavio Paz, *Primera instancia* (Mexico City, 1993), p. 28.

2 Taking a Stand, 1937–43

1 Guillermo Sheridan, *Poeta con paisaje: Ensayos sobre la vida de Octavio Paz* (Mexico City, 2004), pp. 163–4.

2 Mentioned in Enrico Mario Santí, 'Primeras palabras sobre Primeras Letras', *Insula*, nos 532–3 ([Madrid] April–May 1991), pp. 6–7.

3 Octavio Paz, *Entre la piedra y la flor* (Mexico City, 1941).

4 Pablo Neruda, *Memoirs* (London, 2004).

5 Sheridan, *Poeta con paisaje*, pp. 182–4.

6 Claire Cea, *Octavio Paz – 'Poetes d'aujourdhui 126'* (Paris, 1965), p. 22.

7 Octavio Paz, *Itinerary* (London, 1999), p. 49.

8 Elena Poniatowska, *Las palabras del árbol* (Barcelona, 1998), p. 30.

9 Octavio Paz, 'Piedra de sol', in *Collected Poems 1957–1987* (Manchester, 1988), pp. 16–19.

10 Sheridan, *Poeta con paisaje*, p. 295.

11 Interview with the author.

12 Octavio Paz, *Bajo tu clara sombra y otros poemas sobre España* (Valencia, 1937).

13 Jason Wilson, *Octavio Paz* (Boston, 1986), p. 17.

14 Sheridan, *Poeta con paisaje*, p. 305.

15 Rita Guibert, *Seven Voices* (New York, 1973), pp. 212–13.

16 Sheridan, *Poeta con paisaje*, pp. 309–10.

17 Cea, *Octavio Paz*, p. 23.

18 Poniatowska, *Las palabras del árbol*, p. 31.

19 Wilson, *Octavio Paz*, p. 16.

20 Cea, *Octavio Paz*, pp. 28–9.

21 Octavio Paz, *Peras del olmo*, quoted in Cea, *Octavio Paz*, p. 27.

22 Alberto Ruy Sánchez, *Una introducción a Octavio Paz* (Mexico 1990), p. 45.

23 Octavio Paz, *Libertad bajo palabra* (Mexico City, 1949), p. 36.

24 Octavio Paz, *Entre la piedra y flor* (Mexico City, 1941).

25 Octavio Paz, *Obra poética (1935–1988)* (Barcelona, 1990), pp. 785–6.

26 Quoted in Wilson, *Octavio Paz*, p. 9.

27 Ibid.

28 Quoted in Sheridan, *Poeta con paisaje*, p. 26.

29 Cea, *Octavio Paz*, p. 43.

30 Enrico Mario Santí, *Primeras Letras (1931–43)* (Barcelona, 1988), p. 24.

31 Paz, *A la orilla del mundo* (Mexico City, 1942).

32 Sheridan, *Poeta con paisaje*, p. 422.

33 Santí, *Primeras Letras*.

34 Paz, 'El desconocido', in *Libertad bajo palabra*, p. 97.

35 Octavio Paz, *El laberinto de la soledad* (Mexico City, 1950; 2nd edn with addition of *La dialectica de la soledad*, Mexico City, 1959).

36 Paz, *Itinerary*, p. 26.

3 New Departures, 1943–53

1 Quoted in Guillermo Sheridan, *Poeta con paisaje: Ensayos sobre la vida de Octavio Paz* (Mexico City, 2004), p. 433.
2 See Reference 14 for Chapter 1.
3 Octavio Paz, *Itinerary* (London, 1999), p. 19.
4 Enrico Mario Santí, *Octavio Paz, El laberinto de la soledad* (Madrid, 1997), pp. 36–7.
5 Octavio Paz, *El laberinto de la soledad* (Mexico City, 1950).
6 Quoted in Jason Wilson, *Octavio Paz* (Boston, 1986), p. 28.
7 Sheridan, *Poeta con paisaje*, p. 437.
8 Octavio Paz, *Libertad bajo palabra* (Mexico City, 1949).
9 *Memorias y palabras* (Barcelona, 1999), p. 231.
10 Quoted in Guillermo Sheridan, *Cuadernos hispanomericanos* (Madrid, 2005), p. 27.
11 Quoted in Sheridan, *Poeta con paisaje*, pp. 445–6.
12 Octavio Paz, *Alternating Current*, quoted in Jason Wilson, *Octavio Paz* (Boston, 1986), p. 38.
13 Paz, *Libertad bajo palabra*. A reworked version of the volume was published as *Libertad bajo palabra: obra poética (1935–1957)* (Mexico City, 1960).
14 Octavio Paz, *El laberinto de la soledad* (Mexico City, 1950). Second edition, with the addition of *La dialectica de la soledad* (Mexico City, 1959).
15 Octavio Paz, *¿Aguila o sol?* (Mexico City, 1951).
16 Santí, *Octavio Paz*, p. 44.
17 Octavio Paz, *Los hijos del limo* (Barcelona, 1974).
18 Octavio Paz and Julián Ríos, *Solo a dos voces* (Barcelona, 1973), p. 53.
19 Santí, *Octavio Paz*, pp. 147–8.
20 Julián Ríos and Octavio Paz, *Solo a dos voces* (Barcelona, 1973), p. 58.
21 Quoted in Santí, *Octavio Paz*, pp. 43–4.
22 Santí, *Octavio Paz*, p. 49.
23 Santí, *Octavio Paz*, p. 47.
24 Octavio Paz, *An Anthology of Mexican Poetry*, trans. Samuel Beckett (Bloomington, IN, 1958).
25 Octavio Paz, *La estación violenta* (Mexico City, 1958).
26 Sheridan, *Poeta con paisaje*, p. 449.

27 Letter to Reyes, quoted in Sheridan, *Poeta con paisaje*, p. 450.

28 Interview with Alfred MacAdam, *Vuelta*, xv (December 1991), p. 16.

4 Reaching Out, 1953–69

1 For a vivid description of this period and its politics, see Enrique Krauze, *La Presidencia Imperial* (Barcelona, 1997), pp. 89–187.

2 Jason Wilson, *Octavio Paz* (Boston, 1986), pp. 77–8.

3 Enrico Mario Santí, *Octavio Paz, El laberinto de la soledad* (Madrid, 1997), p. 54.

4 Octavio Paz, *Semillas para un himno* (Mexico City, 1954).

5 Wilson, *Octavio Paz*, p. 79.

6 The relation between the two writers has not always been friendly. Paz has criticized Fuentes for being too uncritical towards the revolutionary left in Mexico and elsewhere in Latin America; for his part Fuentes wrote movingly about the poet after his death, although admitting they had 'different concepts of life and society' (*New Perspectives Quarterly*, Summer 1988, p. 5).

7 Elena Poniatowska, *Octavio Paz, Las palabras del árbol* (Barcelona, 1998).

8 Poniatowksa, *Octavio Paz*, p. 49.

9 Quoted in Poniatowska, *Octavio Paz*, p. 57.

10 Octavio Paz, *La estación violenta* (Mexico City, 1958).

11 Paz, *La estación violenta*, p. 42.

12 Guillermo Sheridan, *Poeta con paisaje: Ensayos sobre la vida de Octavio Paz* (Mexico City, 2004), p. 459.

13 For a detailed discussion of the play and its relation to the Hawthorne story, see Raúl Chavarri, *Cuadernos Hispanoamericanos*, 343–5 (January–March 1979), pp. 503–24.

14 Octavio Paz, *El arco y la lira* (Mexico City, 1956).

15 Rafael Argullol, 'Poesía y enigma', *Insula*, 532–3 ([Madrid] April–May 1991), p. 15.

16 Michael Hamburger *The Truth of Poetry* (London, 1970), pp. 40–41.

17 Pere Gimferrer, *Lecturas de Octavio Paz* (Barcelona, 1980), p. 23.

18 Poniatowksa, *Octavio Paz*, p. 46.

19 In Alfredo Roggiano, ed., *Octavio Paz* (Madrid, 1979), pp. 111–24.

20 Octavio Paz, *Piedra de sol* (Mexico City, 1957).

21 The Aztec calendar or sunstone is now housed in the Museum of Anthropology, Mexico City. Its precise significance is still a matter of considerable debate.

22 Born in Rome in 1926, Bona Tibertelli De Pisis was the niece of the 'Pittura Metafisica'-style artist Filippo De Pisis. She took up painting during the Second World War, met the French writer André Pieyre de Mandiargues during a trip to Paris, and married him in 1950. As well as her paintings, drawings and 'soft-art' pieces, she wrote a short novel, *La Cafarde,* autobiographical fragments under the title *Bonaventure,* and a memoir of her childhood in pre-war Italy, *Vivre en herbe.* She died in the year 2000.

23 Octavio Paz, *Libertad bajo palabra* (Mexico City, 1960).

24 Octavio Paz, 'Los pasos contados', *Camp de l'arpa, revista de literatura,* no. 74 ([Barcelona] April 1980) p. 62.

25 Octavio Paz and Pere Gimferrer, *Memorias y palabras* (Barcelona, 1999), Letter 46, pp. 80–83.

26 Sheridan, *Poeta con paisaje*, pp. 464–6.

27 Ibid., p. 470.

28 Octavio Paz, *Salamandra (1958–1961)* (Mexico City, 1962).

29 Octavio Paz and Julián Ríos, *Solo a dos voces* (Barcelona, 1973), p. 53.

30 Wilson, *Octavio Paz*, p. 99.

31 Claire Céa, *Octavio Paz* (Paris, 1965), pp. 82–3. A further sign of Paz's growing international recognition was the award from Belgium in 1964 of that country's *Grand Prix International de Poésie*, all the more appreciated by Paz because previous winners included Jorge Guillén and Giuseppe Ungaretti.

32 Quoted in Sheridan, *Poeta con paisaje*, p. 481.

33 Julián Ríos and Octavio Paz, *Solo a dos voces* (Barcelona, 1973), p. 54. In the 1980s the two men disagreed sharply over the Sandinista Revolution in Nicaragua, which Paz condemned but Cortázar supported.

34 John Cage, *A Year From Monday* (London, 1968), p. 69. The title of Cage's essays also comes from a meeting with Paz, as the American writer explains in the foreword: 'It was a Saturday; there were six of us having dinner in a restaurant on the Hudson north of Newburgh; we arranged to meet in Mexico ... three had been in Mexico and were delighted at the prospect of returning; one was born there but hadn't

been there for five years; his wife, whom he married in India, like me
has never been there', p. x.

35 Octavio Paz, *Ladera este (1962–1968)* (Mexico City, 1969).

36 Octavio Paz, *Cuadrivio* (Mexico City, 1965).

37 Octavio Paz, *Blanco* (Mexico City, 1967).

38 Ríos and Paz, *Solo a dos voces*, p. 53.

39 Enrico Mario Santí, *Archivo blanco* (Mexico City, 1995), pp. 147–8, 151–2.

40 Octavio Paz, *Collected Poems, 1957–1987* (Manchester, 1988), p. 210.

41 See Nicholas Caistor, *Mexico City, a Cultural and Literary Companion*
(Oxford, 2000), pp. 131–8.

42 Sheridan, *Poeta con paisaje*, pp. 485–95.

43 See Pere Gimferrer, *Octavio Paz, memorias y palabras* (Barcelona,
1999), pp. 29–30.

44 Recent documents show that the two women may have been paid by
the Mexican government to make these declarations against him. See
Carlos Landeros, *Yo, Elena Garro* (Mexico City, 2007), pp. 73–111.

45 Octavio Paz, *Posdata* (Mexico City, 1970). The book was an immediate
bestseller, and by 1980 fourteen editions of it had appeared in
Mexico.

5 Bringing it all Back Home, 1969–90

1 Quoted in Enrique Krauze, *La presidencia imperial* (Barcelona, 1997),
p. 381.

2 Octavio Paz, *Los hijos del limo* (Barcelona, 1974).

3 Octavio Paz, *El mono gramático* (Barcelona, 1974).

4 English version, translated by Helen Lane, published by Peter Owen
(London, 1989). The page references are to this edition.

5 Octavio Paz, *The Monkey Grammarian* (London, 1989), p. 50.

6 Paz, *Monkey Grammarian*, pp. 110–11.

7 Octavio Paz, *Discos visuales* (Mexico City, 1968).

8 Octavio Paz, *Topoemas* (Mexico City, 1971).

9 Octavio Paz (with Jacques Roubaud, Edoardo Sanguinetti, and
Charles Tomlinson), *Renga* (Mexico City, 1972).

10 Octavio Paz and Charles Tomlinson, *Airborn/Hijos del aire* (Mexico
City, 1981).

11 Quoted in Enrique Krauze, *La presidencia imperial*, p. 404.

12 Paz's insistence on this score led to a distancing from novelist Carlos Fuentes, whom he had known since the 1950s. Fuentes was convinced that President Echeverría's wishes to 'modernize' the revolution were sincere, and threw his weight behind the system. In 1975 he followed the same diplomatic path as Paz, when he was appointed ambassador in Paris on the personal recommendation of the president.

13 Quoted in Antonio Ruy Sánchez, *Una introducción a Octavio Paz* (Mexico City, 1990), p. 105.

14 Octavio Paz, *Traducción: literatura y literalidad* (Barcelona, 1971).

15 Paz, *Los hijos del limo*.

16 José Quiroga, *Understanding Octavio Paz* (Columbia, SC, 1999), p. 107.

17 Octavio Paz, *Pasado en claro* (Mexico City, 1975).

18 Mexican TV programme, *Itinerario*, 1989.

19 Octavio Paz, *Collected Poems, 1957–1987* (Manchester, 1988), p. 432.

20 Octavio Paz, *Vuelta* (Barcelona, 1976).

21 For a measured discussion of the figure of Paz as a liberal intellectual in these years, see Armando González Torres, *Las guerras culturales de Octavio Paz* (Puebla, 2002). Perhaps the most interesting book criticizing Paz's position is Jorge Aguilar Mora, *La divina pareja: Historia y mito en Octavio Paz* (Mexico City, 1978).

22 Octavio Paz, *El ogro filantrópico: historia y política 1971–1978* (Mexico City, 1979).

23 Octavio Paz, *Poemas (1935–1975)* (Barcelona, 1979).

24 Octavio Paz, *Sor Juana Inés de la Cruz o las trampas de la fe* (Barcelona, 1982).

25 Cf. Pedro Serrano, 'La torre y el caracol', *Fractal*, 6 (Autumn 1997).

26 Quoted in Georgina Sabat de Rivers, 'Octavio Paz ante Sor Juana Inés de la Cruz', *Modern Language Notes*, C/2 (March 1985), pp. 417–23.

27 Ibid.

28 See Torres, *Las guerras culturales de Octavio Paz*, p. 108.

29 Octavio Paz, *Tiempo nublado* (Barcelona, 1983).

30 Enrique Krauze, *Travesía liberal* (Mexico City, 2003)

31 Octavio Paz, *México en la obra de Octavio Paz* (Mexico City, 1987), 3 vols.

32 Pere Gimferrer, *Octavio Paz, memorias y palabras* (Barcelona, 1999), p. 324.

33 Octavio Paz, *Árbol adentro* (Barcelona, 1987).

34 Octavio Paz, *Pequeña crónica de grandes días* (Mexico City, 1990).
35 Octavio Paz, *La otra voz: poesía y fin de siglo* (Barcelona, 1990).

6 Consuming Fires, 1990–98

1 Octavio Paz, *In Search of the Present: Nobel Lecture.* Available at http://www.nobel.se/literature/laureates/1990/paz-lecture.html.
2 Octavio Paz, *La llama doble, Amor y erotismo* (Madrid, 1993).
3 Octavio Paz, *The Double Flame* (London, 1995), p. ix.
4 Paz, *The Double Flame*, p. 113.
5 Octavio Paz, *Vislumbres de la India* (Barcelona, 1995).
6 Lawrence Saez, 'Octavio Paz 1914–1998', *Journal of Asian Studies*, LVII/4 (November 1998), pp. 1241–3.
7 Octavio Paz, *Itinerario* (Barcelona, 1994), translated into English as *Itinerary* (London, 1999). The quotations are from the English edition.
8 Octavio Paz, 'Chiapas: nudo ciego o tabla de salvación', *La Jornada* (23–24 January 1994).
9 Armando González Torres, *Las guerras culturales de Octavio Paz* (Puebla, 2002), p. 133.
10 Ilan Stavans, 'Of Arms and the Essayist', *Transition*, LX (1993), pp. 102–17.
11 Octavio Paz, 'Respuesta y reconciliación (Diálogo con Francisco de Quevedo)', *Vuelta*, CCLIX (June 1998), pp. 6–9.

Select Bibliography

Poetry Collections in Spanish

Luna silvestre (Mexico City: Fábula, 1933)
¡No pasarán! (Mexico City: Simbad, 1936)
Raíz del hombre (Mexico City: Simbad, 1937)
Bajo tu clara sombra y otros poemas sobre España (Valencia: Ediciones
    Españolas, 1937)
Entre la piedra y la flor (Mexico City: Nueva Voz, 1941)
A la orilla del mundo (Mexico City: ARS, 1942)
Libertad bajo palabra (Mexico City: Fondo de Cultura Económica, 1949)
Semillas para un himno (Mexico City: Fondo de Cultura Económica, 1954)
Piedra de sol (Mexico City: Fondo de Cultura Económica, 1957)
La estación violenta (Mexico City: Fondo de Cultura Económica, 1958)
Salamandra (1958–1961) (Mexico City: Joaquín Mortiz, 1962)
Viento entero (Delhi: The Caxton Press, 1965)
Blanco (Mexico City: Joaquín Mortiz, 1967)
Discos visuales (Mexico City: Ediciones ERA, 1968)
Ladera este (1962–1968) (Mexico City: Joaquín Mortiz, 1969)
La centena (1935–1968) (Barcelona: Barral, 1969)
*Topoemas (*Mexico City: Ediciones ERA, 1971)
Renga (Mexico City: Joaquín Mortiz, 1972) Collective poem with Jacques
    Roubaud, Edoardo Sanguinetti and Charles Tomlinson)
Pasado en claro (Mexico City: Fondo de Cultura Económica, 1975)
Vuelta (Barcelona: Seix Barral, 1976)
Hijos del aire/Airborn. Con Charles Tomlinson (Mexico City: Martín Pescador,
    1979)
Poemas (1935–1975) (Barcelona: Seix Barral, 1979)

Árbol adentro (1976–1987) (Barcelona: Seix Barral, 1987)

Lo mejor de Octavio Paz. El fuego de cada día. Selection, prologue and notes
  by the author (Barcelona: Seix Barral, 1989)

Prose Poetry in Spanish

¿Águila o sol? (Mexico City: Fondo de Cultura Económica, 1951)

El mono gramático (Barcelona: Seix Barral, 1974)

Theatre

La hija de Rappaccini (México) in *Revista Mexicana de Literatura*, 7
  (September–October 1956), and in *Poemas* (1979)

Essays

El laberinto de la soledad (Mexico City: Cuadernos Americanos, 1950);
  (2nd edn, Fondo de Cultura Económica, 1959)

El arco y la lira (Mexico City: Fondo de Cultura Económica, 1956)

Las peras del olmo (Mexico City: UNAM, 1957)

Cuadrivio (Mexico City: Joaquín Mortiz, 1965)

Los signos en rotación (Buenos Aires: Sur, 1965)

Puertas al campo (Mexico City: UNAM, 1966)

Claude Lévi-Strauss o el nuevo festín de Esopo (Mexico City: Joaquín Mortiz,
  1967)

Corriente alterna (Mexico City: Siglo XXI, 1967)

Marcel Duchamp o el castillo de la pureza (Mexico City: Ediciones ERA,
  1968); later included in *Apariencia desnuda; la obra de Marcel
  Duchamp* (Mexico City: Ediciones ERA 1973)

Conjunciones y disyunciones (Mexico City: Joaquín Mortiz, 1969)

México: la última década (Austin: Institute of Latin American Studies,
  University of Texas, 1969)

Posdata (Mexico City: Siglo XXI, 1970)

Las cosas en su sitio: sobre la literatura española del siglo xx. With Juan
  Marichal (Mexico City: Finisterre, 1971)

Los signos en rotación y otros ensayos. Introduced by Carlos Fuentes
  (Madrid: Alianza Editorial, 1971)
Traducción: literatura y literalidad (Barcelona: Tusquets Editores, 1971)
El signo y el garabato (Mexico City: Joaquín Mortiz, 1973)
Solo a dos voces. With Julián Rios (Barcelona: Lumen, 1973)
Teatro de signos/Transparencias. Edited by Julián Rios (Madrid:
  Fundamentos, 1974)
La búsqueda del comienzo (Madrid: Fundamentos, 1974)
Los hijos del limo: del romanticismo a la vanguardia (Barcelona: Seix Barral,
  1974)
Xavier Villaurrutia en persona y en obra (Mexico City: Fondo de Cultura
  Económica, 1978)
El ogro filantrópico: historia y política (1971–1978) (Mexico City: Joaquín
  Mortiz, 1979)
In/mediaciones (Barcelona: Seix Barral, 1979)
México en la obra de Octavio Paz. Edited and with an Introduction by Luis
  Mario Schneider (Mexico City: Promociones Editoriales Mexicanas,
  1979)
Sor Juana Inés de la Cruz o las trampas de la fe (Mexico City: Fondo de
  Cultura Económica 1982; Barcelona: Seix Barral, 1982)
Tiempo nublado (Barcelona: Seix Barral, 1983)
Sombras de obras (Barcelona: Seix Barral, 1983)
Hombres en su siglo y otros ensayos (Barcelona: Seix Barral, 1984)
Pasión crítica: conversaciones con Octavio Paz. Edited by Hugo J. Verani
  (Barcelona: Seix Barral, 1985)
México en la obra de Octavio Paz, 3 volúmes:
    I. El peregrino en su patria. Historia y política de México.
    II. Generaciones y semblanzas. Escritores y letras de México.
    III. Los privilegios de la vista. Arte de México.
  Edited by Luis Mario Schneider and Octavio Paz (Mexico City: Fondo
  de Cultura Económica, 1987)
Primeras Letras (1931-1943). Edited and Introduced by Enrico Mario Santi
  (Barcelona: Seix Barral, 1988, and Mexico City: Vuelta, 1988)
Poesía, mito, revolución. With speeches by François Mitterrand, Alain
  Peyrefitte, Pierre Godefroy. Alexis de Tocqueville Prize (Mexico City:
  Vuelta, 1989)
La otra voz. Poesía y fin de siglo (Barcelona: Seix Barral, 1990)

Anthologies and Collections edited by Paz

Anthologie de la poésie mexicaine. Edited with an introduction by Octavio
 Paz, with a note by Paul Claudel (Paris: Editions Nagel [Col. UNESCO],
 1952)

Anthology of Mexican Poetry. Edited with an introduction by Octavio Paz
 with a note by C. M. Bowra, and English translation by Samuel
 Beckett (Bloomington, IN, 1958)

Basho, Matsuo. Sendas de Oku. Translated by Eikichi Hayashiya and
 Octavio Paz, with an introduction by Octavio Paz (México: UNAM,
 1957, and Seix Barral, 1970)

Laurel: Antología de la poesía moderna en lengua española. Edited by Xavier
 Villaurrutia, Emilio Prados, Juan Gil-Albert and Octavio Paz (Mexico
 City: Editorial Séneca, 1941)

Pessoa, Fernando. Edited, translated and with an introduction by Octavio
 Paz (Mexico City: UNAM, 1962)

Poesía en movimiento (México: 1915–1966). Edited by Octavio Paz, Alí
 Chumacero, Homero Aridjis and José Emilio Pacheco (Mexico City:
 Siglo XXI, 1966)

Versiones y diversiones. Poetry translations (Mexico City: Joaquín Mortiz, 1974)

Paz also compiled and edited his complete works in 14 volumes: *Obras
 completas* (Barcelona: Círculo de Lectores, 1992)

Works by Octavio Paz in English

Selected Poems of Octavio Paz: A Bilingual Edition, trans. Muriel Rukeyser
 (Bloomington, IN, 1963)

The Other Mexico (New York, 1972)

Alternating Current (New York, 1973)

*The Bow and the Lyre: (El arco y la lira), the Poem, the Poetic Revelation, Poetry
 and History,* trans. Ruth L. C. Simms (Austin, TX, 1973)

Early Poems, 1935–1955, trans. from the Spanish by Muriel Rukeyser and
 other poets (Bloomington, IN, 1974)

The Siren & the Seashell and Other Essays on Poets and Poetry, trans. Lysander
 Kemp and Margaret Sayers Peden (Austin, TX, 1976)

Marcel Duchamp: *Appearance Stripped Bare*, trans. Rachel Phillips and
　　Donald Gardner (New York, 1978)

The Monkey Grammarian, trans. from the Spanish by Helen R. Lane (New
　　York, 1981)

Selected Poems, ed. Eliot Weinberger; trans. from the Spanish by G. Aroul
　　et al. (New York, 1984)

The Labyrinth of Solitude: *Life and Thought in Mexiko*, trans. Lysander Kemp
　　(Harmondsworth, 1985)

One Earth, Four or Five Worlds: *Reflections on Contemporary History*, trans.
　　Helen R. Lane (New York, 1985)

On Poets and Others, trans. Michael Schmidt (New York, 1986)

Sor Juana or, The Traps of Faith, trans. Margaret Sayers Peden (Cambridge,
　　MA, 1988)

The Collected Poems: *1957–1987*, ed. and trans. Eliot Weinberger; with
　　additional translations by Elizabeth Bishop (Manchester, 1988)

¿Águila o sol?: Eagle or Sun?, trans. from the Spanish by Eliot Weinberger
　　(London, 1990)

Convergences : *Essays on Art and Literature*, trans. from the Spanish by
　　Helen R. Lane (London, 1990)

The Other Voice: *Essays on Modern Poetry*, trans. from the Spanish by
　　Helen R. Lane (New York, 1991)

In Search of the Present: *Nobel Lecture, 1990* (San Diego, 1991)

The Double Flame: *Essays on Love and Eroticism*, trans. from the Spanish by
　　Helen Lane (London, 1996)

In Light of India: *Essays*, trans. from the Spanish by Eliot Weinberger (New
　　York, 1997)

Itinerary, trans. with notes and an afterword by Jason Wilson (London, 1999)

Versiones y diversiones. Bilingual edition (Barcelona: Galaxia Gutenberg;
　　Círculo de Lectores, 2000)

The most complete bibliography of Paz's work is Hugo J. Verani, *Bibliografia
　　crítica de Octavio Paz, 1931–1996* (Mexico City: El Colegio Nacional, 1997)

Books wholly or partly about Octavio Paz

Aguilar Mora, Jorge, *La divina pareja: Historia y mito en Octavio Paz*
　　(Mexico City, 1978)

Bloom, Harold, ed., *Octavio Paz* (Philadelphia, 2002)

Brotherston, Gordon, *Latin American Poetry, Origins and Presence* (Cambridge, 1975)

Céa, Claire, *Octavio Paz – 'Poetes d'aujourd'hui no. 126'* (Paris, 1965)

Chiles, Francis, *Octavio Paz: The Mythic Dimension* (New York, 1987)

Cuadernos Hispanoamericanos, nos. 343–5 (January–March 1979), *Homenaje a Octavio Paz*

Díaz, Susana *(Per)versiones y convergencias* (Madrid, 2005)

Feinstein, Adam, *Pablo Neruda: A Passion for Life* (London, 2004)

Garro, Elena, *Memorias de España 1937* (Mexico City, 1992)

Gimferrer, Pere, *Lecturas de Octavio Paz* (Barcelona, 1980)

——, *Octavio Paz, memorias y palabras* (Barcelona, 1999)

González Rojo, Enrique, *Cuando el rey se hace cortesano: Octavio Paz y el salinismo* (Mexico, 1990)

González Torres, Armando, *Las guerras culturales de Octavio Paz* (Mexico City, 2002)

Gradiva, 6–7 ([París] February 1975). Homage to Octavio Paz

Grenier, Yvon, *From Art to Politics: Octavio Paz and the Pursuit of Freedom* (Mexico City, Boulder, CO, and Oxford, 2001)

Guibert, Rita, *Seven Voices: Seven Latin American Writers Talk to Rita Guibert* (New York, 1973)

Hamburger, Michael, *The Truth of Poetry* (London, 1969)

Ivask, Ivar, *The Perpetual Present: The Poetry and Prose of Octavio Paz* (Norman, OK, 1973)

Krauze, Enrique, *Travesía liberal* (Mexico City, 2003)

Landeros, Carlos, *Yo, Elena Garro* (Mexico City, 2007)

Magis, Carlos, *La poesía hermética de Octavio Paz* (Mexico City, 1978)

Medina, Rubén, *Autor, autoridad y autorización: Escritura y poética de Octavio Paz* (Mexico City, 1999)

Orfila, Arnaldo, *Cartas cruzadas* (Mexico City, 2005)

Peralta, Braulio, *El poeta en su tierra: diálogos con Octavio Paz* (Mexico City, 1996)

Phillips, Rachel, *The Poetic Modes of Octavio Paz* (Oxford, 1972)

Polizzotti, Mark, *Revolution of the Mind: The Life of André Breton* (New York, 1995)

Poniatowska, Elena, *Las palabras del árbol* (Barcelona, 1998)

Quiroga, José, *Understanding Octavio Paz* (Columbia, SC, 1999)

Ríos, Julián and Octavio Paz, *Solo a dos voces* (Barcelona, 1973)

Rodríguez Ledesma, Xavier, *El pensamiento político de Octavio Paz* (Mexico City, 1996)

Ruy Sánchez, Alberto, *Una introducción a Octavio Paz* (Mexico City, 1990)

Santí, Enrico Mario, *Primeras letras (1931–43)* (Barcelona, 1988),

——, *El acto de las palabras: Estudios y diálogos con Octavio Paz* (Mexico City, 1999)

Sheridan, Guillermo, *Poeta con paisaje: Ensayos sobre la vida de Octavio Paz* (Mexico City, 2004)

Stanton, Anthony, *Correspondencia Alfonso Reyes/Octavio Paz (1939–1959)* (Mexico City, 1998)

Wilson, Jason, *Octavio Paz: A Study of his Poetics* (Cambridge, 1979)

——, *Octavio Paz* (Boston, MA, 1986)

Xirau, Ramón, *Octavio Paz: El sentido de la palabra* (Mexico City, 1970)

Zaid, Gabriel, *De los libros al poder* (Mexico City, 1998)

Acknowledgements

Many people in Mexico and Britain have helped with suggestions or ideas for the production of this book. Thanks especially to Margo Glanz, Elena Poniatowksa and Guillermo Sheridan in Mexico; to Amanda Hopkinson (as ever), Professor Jason Wilson in Britain, and to Vivian Constantinopoulos at Reaktion Books for her patience and encouragement.

Photo Acknowledgements

The author and publishers wish to express their thanks to the following sources of illustrative material and/or permission to reproduce it (some locations of artworks are also given below):

Photo Lola Alvarez Bravo: p. 57; photo Julio Etchart: p. 6; photo Pilar Fernández: p. 119; photos Instituto Nacional de Antropologia e Historia, Fototeca Nacional, Pachuca, Mexico: pp. 14, 18, 19, 34, 49, 79; University of Essex, Latin American Art Collection: p. 70; courtesy Jason Wilson: p. 117.